THE WAY WE WERE

Paul Burrell served Diana, Princess of Wales, as her faithful butler from 1987 until her death in 1997. He was much more than an employee: he was her right-hand man, confidant and friend. She described him as 'the only man she ever trusted'.

In this remarkable and intimate book, Paul Burrell opens the door to Kensington Palace to provide a unique, visual tour. Using previously unseen interior photographs, the reader is led inside the world of Princess Diana—room by room, memory-by-memory.

The Way We Were reflects upon, remembers and celebrates the late Diana, Princess of Wales, and captures her vivacity and love of life.

THE WAY WE WERE

WERE

Remembering Diana

Paul Burrell

WINDSOR
PARAGON

First published 2006
by
HarperCollins
This Large Print edition published 2007
by
BBC Audiobooks Ltd by arrangement with
HarperCollins Publishers

Hardcover ISBN: 978 1 405 61704 8
Softcover   ISBN: 978 1 405 61705 5

All photographs have been supplied by the author,
with the exception of the following:
p137 (centre left) David Cheskin/PA/Empics
p141 (top) Martin Keene/PA/Empics
p141 (bottom) PA/Empics
p144 (top) Martin Keene/PA/Empics
p144 (bottom) Fiona Hanson/PA/Empics

British Library Cataloguing in Publication Data available

Printed and bound in Great Britain by
Antony Rowe Ltd., Chippenham, Wiltshire

In memory of two women
who taught me so much about life,

my mother and the boss

I have to go now to the stars. And one day, when you look at the stars, you will remember me.

as quoted by Diana, Princess of Wales, in 1996, from *The Little Prince*.

CONTENTS

INTRODUCTION

In July 2006 I found myself standing inside Kensington Palace, and Diana, Princess of Wales was there once more, with her warm smile and infectious giggle.

I was nothing but a visitor, one of thousands of tourists who pass through those ornate black and gold gates in London W8, and the boss was nothing but her own iconic image, looking down from every wall; her spirit and sense of fun captured perfectly by photographer Mario Testino. It's never easy returning to KP where I worked and lived as butler to the princess, but I had to see Mario's unique tribute, which portrays her like no one ever has before: at her happiest, most relaxed, most radiant, most natural. For me, they show 'Diana, the woman at home' not 'Diana, Princess of Wales on duty'. This was the princess I knew, and how I remember her; the princess Mario wanted the world to see, as if each person who viewed those photos was sitting on the sofa chatting to her. As he did. As I did, during ten years of service at her side.

In his mesmerizing photos, she wore no shoes, no jewellery and little makeup as she sprawled across a sofa, or sat on the floorboards, laughing.

'Laughter, laughter, laughter—that's what the day was all about, Paul. I had such fun!' she said. It is a vivid memory for me because I was at KP in 1997 when 'the boss' returned home from Mario's studio and what had been her final photo shoot—for *Vanity Fair*. 'I've never felt so relaxed,' she went on. She'd had such fun, and was soaring with the confidence Mario had instilled in her, which brought out the best in her for the photos.

I remember the day when, at last, a Kodak box of 8 x 10" prints arrived at the front door. The princess couldn't wait to see them, and I helped her spread more than fifty images across the sitting-room carpet. Then we knelt to scan each shot.

'This is you! He's got you!' I told her.

'Do you think so?' she said, with the sharp intake of breath that punctuated her conversations. 'Is that *really* me?' She giggled, embarrassed to have invited a compliment.

Typically, she allowed me to choose my favourites and ensured I received my own Mario Testino collection of the shots she had discarded. The exhibition, almost ten years later, was important because it illustrated the princess as the world deserved to see her; a side of her that few were privileged to know. In that respect, Mario did her millons of fans, and her memory, a true service.

An appropriate and fitting tribute to Diana, Princess of Wales was long overdue, something more significant than Hyde Park's water memorial, which certainly doesn't do justice to her memory. That's why it is a shame that Mario's exhibition isn't permanent because it is everything that a tribute should be.

Even though I'd seen every image before during my exclusive preview at KP, I wasn't prepared for their impact when I entered the exhibition. It was their sheer size, larger than life, that struck me. The princess dominated the place.

Photographs and words capture memories, and I am writing this commemorative book to give you an insight into the privileged life I shared with the princess, in memory and celebration of her. I have included my own photographs of Apartments 8 and 9, to form a visual tribute that the Royal Family accorded to the late Queen Mother and Princess Margaret, but not the princess.

I took photographs of each room—and of her jewellery—in September 1997, and I'm sharing them with you, opening the door as Butler to show how this iconic royal once lived. I hope my words and pictures evoke powerful memories. I'm no Mario Testino but he and I share the same aim: to remember a unique and remarkable woman—especially as the long overdue and much delayed British inquest into her death in Paris, on 31 August 1997, is now in view. Over the past two years, I have assisted Scotland Yard officers, investigating on behalf of the coroner, as much as I can. I have spent many hours with them and provided statements and suggestions to aid them in their pursuit of the truth as to what really happened. It has been a thorough investigation, there is a fear that, in the process, Diana, Princess of Wales, might be remembered for all the wrong reasons, her character so scrutinized that it is in danger of being distorted; that her warmth, spirit, vivacity and good work will be lost and the concerns she harboured for her safety are misrepresented.

So, I have written this book to keep at the forefront of our minds a true memory of the boss. I hope it shines through these pages, and continues to shine after the inquest process, whatever is said, whatever is alleged, whatever is decided. When it is over, we will be approaching the tenth anniversary of her death—a true time for remembrance and reflection.

I am aware that my intention in writing this book may be misrepresented and misjudged by the media and system that attacked me for my first book, *A Royal Duty*, which appeared in 2003. It was portrayed as 'a betrayal' but, as more than 93,000 letters to me have confirmed, it was a tribute, as I intend this book to be. I hope people will read *The Way We Were* and judge it on its tone and content, not on its media portrayal. I have always said that I will stand for ever in the princess's corner and shout on her behalf, and there seems no better time to remember her than now—as vividly as we knew her before that terrible autumn of 1997.

My memories don't mellow with time. If I close my eyes, I can still smell the lilies in the sitting room, hear the Victorian gas lamps hissing in the courtyard at KP or the grandfather clock ticking on the stairs. I can still see the princess in the drawing room, playing Rachmaninov's Piano Concerto No. 2, I can still see her sitting in a window seat on a summer's day, the sun on her face, eyes closed, tucking her hair behind an ear.

As her butler, I invite you to step inside a unique world. This book commemorates the life of the 'People's Princess'. Your princess. My boss.

PAUL BURRELL

BACK HOME

The gold Yale key turned in the lock, and my stomach lurched as the back door of Kensington Palace opened. I stepped inside and walked forward, as the heavy black door slammed behind me, sending an echo throughout the emptiness that lay ahead. It was as dark and gloomy as ever in that part of the palace so I flicked the light switch. Nothing happened. The bulb must have blown, I thought.

Then I looked up to the ceiling and saw that the entire light fitting had been ripped out, leaving only dangling wires. I walked on, my footsteps echoing, to what had been the engine room of the 'home' I called KP, where tradesmen, staff and deliverymen had once busied themselves. I was in the middle of the lobby, once filled with the buzz of the refrigerator, the whirr of the ice-making machine, the swish of the dishwasher, the chatter of people coming and going. Now there was a void. The mail pigeon-holes were empty, black bin bags, empty drawers and chairs lay about, discarded. KP looked as if it had been ransacked by thieves. Apartments 8 and 9 had been reduced to a shell, there wasn't a single hook for my memories.

It was 2002, and I had gone back to the apartments of Diana, Princess of Wales for the first time since I had left them in July 1998 when, even then, they were being emptied. Fine furniture was transferred to the Royal Collection. Jewellery was returned to Buckingham Palace. As the family was entitled to do, Princes William and Harry and the Spencer family had taken some items, and the Crown Estates had reclaimed the property. On the day I moved out, 24 July 1998, the apartments were being stripped. It was too painful for me to witness. I wanted to leave with a mental picture of what had been, dismissing the reality of what was taking place.

In the ensuing four years I steered clear of the palace. I never imagined I'd ever see the day when I'd need to go back. I didn't want to go back. But it became necessary to return 'home' when Scotland Yard and the CPS charged me with theft from the boss's estate—the system's response to my spontaneous protection of her legacy. In preparation for my Old Bailey trial, which ended in acquittal in 2002, I had to walk my legal team through the palace to build up a picture of what life, and my role, had been like.

That day, accompanied by my barrister Lord Carlile, QC, and solicitor Andrew Shaw, I steeled myself for what I knew I would see—the dismantling of the princess's world had long been complete. But I was still unprepared for the devastating scene of erasure and decay that confronted me when I walked up the main staircase, then went from room to room. Each had been stripped with a disregard that said everything about how the princess had been treated in life.

Nothing had been respected. Workmen had moved in, ripping up carpets, tearing down the silk wall panels that had decorated the drawing room and sitting room, leaving the doors of fitted cupboards hanging off their hinges. Even plug sockets had been removed. There were horizontal gaps where the odd floorboard had been pulled up and left propped against a wall. Newspapers were scattered on the floor. A blue mattress was propped against one wall. Junk lay everywhere. And it was dirty. It seemed that the place hadn't been cleaned in the four years since 1998. A layer of dust covered the once polished banisters, giant cobwebs were spun round grubby cornices, and the air was musty. A once pristine home was now as dark and unhealthy as Charles Dickens had depicted Satis House in *Great Expectations.*

Those with no reason to care about the princess's world, and the devastation I saw might have shrugged and said, 'Well, she's dead. It's time to move on. Who cares?' But moving on shouldn't mean forgetting.

I could have cried as I walked round those rooms. It was a stark illustration of how quickly some people had wanted to forget her, how eager some people were to remove every vestige of her.

It also represented a lost opportunity. A potential museum of memories had been wrecked.

After Princess Margaret's death in 2002, the administration of her home, Apartment 1A, was transferred to the care of Historic Royal Palaces so that part of her living quarters could be viewed for educational and exhibition purposes. Today, although the place has been stripped of its furniture, the public has the chance to visualize Princess Margaret's life, and study the photographs of her. Would it not have been possible to do the same with Apartments 8 and 9 five years earlier?

Also, when the Queen Mother died in 2002, the Prince of Wales ensured that there was a fitting tribute to his grandmother: he arranged for the

World of Interiors magazine to photograph the inside of her home to show how she had lived; to capture her way of life, her tastes and style, for posterity. It was published in October 2003.

That is why I've decided to share with you my photographs, taken inside Apartments 8 and 9.

I took them, with my own camera, in the weeks after the princess's death, for purely sentimental reasons—to preserve what had been a special place to me. They also catalogued the precise location of her possessions, which was useful to me in my role as guardian of her world.

Over the years, the photographs have been a comfort, and have helped me remember details and moments that might have blurred with time. Many people from around the world have written to me, or asked me face to face, what life was like with the boss, how she lived, and what her inner sanctum *really* looked like. Well, the photographs in this book provide the answer; you will enjoy a virtual tour of Apartments 8 and 9. They show the rooms as she left them.

Today, Apartment 9, which housed the princess's bedroom, bathroom, dressing room, wardrobe rooms and part of the nursery, provides accommodation for members of the Queen's household. But Apartment 8—the main staircase, sitting room, drawing room, dining room, kitchen and my pantry—remains a shell. I hope my photographs recapture the spirit of this home and offer a vivid image of what life was like with the boss. Her private rooms deserve to be remembered for the vibrancy, drama, laughter, tears and magic of a life lived to the full. That is why, as butler to that residence, I'm opening the doors to show you around. This is the way we were . . .

*   *   *

She called the walled garden her 'little oasis', her place of escape and solitude. There was only one key to the black door set in the surrounding brickwork and, as the resident of Apartments 8 and 9, the princess had exclusive access, shared with me and the gardener. It was the only set of four walls behind which she found complete relaxation and sanctuary, with the sky as a roof.

Almost a decade since her death, my memories of that garden, and life at KP, are as vivid as ever. If I close my eyes, my mind evokes those special years of duty between 1993 and 1997. Her garden was scented, with roses of all colours climbing half-way up the ten-foot-high walls. There was a flowering cherry, a pergola in one corner, a long, rectangular lawn with a wide border, a central oak in which squirrels nested, a potting shed and a dilapidated old greenhouse.

In summer, on blazing hot days, I knew the routine. I can see her now, in a pair of shorts and a vest, and wearing her Versace sunglasses, almost skipping out of the front door, with a pale-blue wicker basket filled with correspondence, books, CDs, a Walkman, a low-factor Clarins suncream and her mobile phone. She never went anywhere without her phone.

Then she'd settle down with her hair tied back. When she was relaxing, in the garden, in the sitting room before bedtime or at breakfast, she scraped back her blonde hair with an elasticated cloth band. She had several, in black, blue and purple. If

9

the world remembers the princess for her signature hairstyle, I remember her for that band! Sometimes, as she talked on the phone, that hairband would be wrapped round her fingers, and she'd toy with it, then put it back on her head.

I never joined the boss in the garden. It was her private time. When that black door swung shut, she was alone, as she wanted to be. Often, she returned to KP with a bunch of roses for a vase on her desk. She never stayed out there long, maybe an hour or two. She was too restless to keep still for longer than that. As much as she portrayed herself as a sun-worshipper, she was too impatient to lie immobile for long. The sun-bed, in half-hour bursts, was more her cup of tea.

If the garden was her sanctuary, Apartments 8 and 9 were the home that was filled with the laughter of the young princes William and Harry, but also the tears and sadness of the boss's well-documented personal strife. The entrance was a set of black double doors, flanked by two giant wooden planters.

One day in early spring, I decided to fill them with rows of hyacinths, like the ones at Windsor Castle planted round the Queen's private entrance, called the 'dog door', because Her Majesty used it when she walked her corgis. In my eleven years' service as footman to the Queen—from 1976 to 1987—the gardeners at Windsor planted row upon row of blue hyacinths, to flower around Easter time, and I was met by their heavenly scent each time I was on corgi-walking duty—up to eight times a day. Those dogs never tired of walks! I suppose I planted the hyacinths because I thought that the scent would be a lovely welcome for visitors to KP. Except one visitor didn't agree. When Prince Charles saw what I had done, he chastised me. He told me it was far too early to plant hyacinths outside. 'It's such a waste, Paul!' he said.

And, of course, he was right. What the prince didn't know about plants and gardening could have been written on the back of his mother's head—on a British postage stamp. I had witnessed his skills in the garden many times during my service as butler to the Prince and Princess of Wales at Highgrove, from 1987 to 1993, so I knew he was talking sense, even if his manner was somewhat brusque. Not that I was going to give him the satisfaction of watching me dig the bulbs out. Instead, each night for the next month, I covered them up with an old bed-sheet to protect them from the frost. I did it my way—after all, it was the boss's home, not his any more. She loved that scent, so maybe I'd got it right, after all.

From the front door of KP, visitors stepped out on to the gravel that surrounded an oval lawn, like a mini-roundabout, with a central flower-bed, overlooked by the first-floor dining-room windows. The princess always drove her BMW in nose first. As soon as she was inside the house, I would nip out with the car keys and turn it round so that it was ready to be driven out the next time she needed it.

About two hundred yards ahead of the door there was a block called the Upper Stables. Staff quarters filled the first floor and Princess Margaret's garage was underneath. To the left, a group of cottages was used by senior members of the Royal Household: Kent Cottage, Nottingham

Cottage and Wren Cottage. To the right, there was a dead end: a towering brick wall with a black door set in it, which led to the State Apartments and the Orangery. The princess used that gate to nip out into Kensington Palace Gardens for a walk, or to go rollerblading at around 8 a.m. when few people were around. To reach it, she had to pass the door to Prince and Princess Michael of Kent's apartments. I occasionally went in for chats with the Portuguese housekeeper, Julia—it was like walking into a full-size doll's house, immaculate and chintzy. Whereas my first impression on walking into Apartments 8 and 9 was of simple elegance: the walls down the narrow entrance corridor, with its barrelled ceiling, were painted primrose yellow and led to an archway into the vestibule where there was a cloakroom. The boss always stopped there on her way out. She would thrust her handbag into my hand and say: 'Wait there—but hum or sing loudly!' Instead, I waited discreetly in the hallway.

Across the vestibule, a doorway opened on to the main staircase, which climbed up then turned at a right angle to the first-floor landing and the boss's private rooms. From that same doorway, six steps dropped down to the right and the butler's pantry. It was there that I often waited for the princess to arrive home, waited for the frosted-glass panes to rattle in the door, those quick, light footsteps on the carpet, as she bounded up the stairs, rushing in like a whirlwind of energy. Moments later the floorboards directly above me would creak, indicating that she was moving between her dressing room, bedroom and sitting room. Those old floorboards often told me her whereabouts and her mood: slow, unhurried movement meant she was relaxed; frantic pacing meant she was in a rush or had taken a phone call that had upset her.

The staircase was wide with a classical white balustrade topped with a varnished, bevelled-edged banister. White garland mouldings fell down the walls from an intricate cornice, and a grandfather clock stood on one of the turns in the stairs. One high window cast daylight over them. On the sill, the boss kept a Steuben crystal vase, a gift from US President Ronald Reagan and his wife Nancy on behalf of the American people, with a scene of the Pilgrim Fathers landing in America carved into it. Sadly, a housekeeper washed it in too hot water and it cracked from base to lip. It was replaced with a hand-blown Venetian crystal lion.

Those stairs are a focal point for my memories. It was there that she stood and did a twirl to show off a new dress or outfit; there that I told her she had never looked so good before she left on that ill-fated excursion with Dodi Al Fayed. It was also the spot from which she would shout, 'Paul, are you there?' In response, I would bolt up to the first floor, past a stunning full-length portrait of her painted by Nelson Shanks. It hung on the wall, adjacent to the grandfather clock, and showed a contemplative princess wearing a diaphanous white blouse, with a ruffed collar and cuffs, and an ankle-length blue taffeta skirt. Around her neck she wore Queen Mary's emerald and diamond choker which the Queen had given her as a wedding present in 1981. The boss felt it rather vain to have such a huge image of herself as a centrepiece on the stairs—at least, she feared

13

others would judge her as vain. I think, though, she was proud of it, even if she didn't let on that she was to too many people. Instead, walking up the stairs with a friend or a visitor, she would ask what they thought of it and, before they had the chance to answer, add, 'It looks like I'm about to jump off a bridge, doesn't it?' That was her way of dealing with self-consciousness. Today, that portrait takes pride of place on a wall at Althorp, the Spencer family home in Northamptonshire.

John Ward sketches also hung on the wall, favoured snapshots from the Waleses' family history: William's christening in the music room at Buckingham Palace, Harry's christening in St George's Chapel, and the Prince and Princess of Wales's wedding day at St Paul's Cathedral. It was on those stairs, beneath those pictures, that we'd sit together, the boss on one step, her butler on the one below, talking through a piece of correspondence she had received, or composing a letter of her own.

As one of the princess's closest friends, Rosa Monckton, wrote in the *Sunday Telegraph* in November 2002, 'When I was in Greece with Diana, we discussed Paul. She . . . told me how he often helped her to write her letters, and they would sit on the stairs together. "What do you think, Rosa—the Princess and Her Butler?"'

I can picture the scene now: the boss sitting down, knees together, on the carpeted step, scribbling words and thoughts on her memo pad or revising a letter, scratching through a sentence or phrase. As she thought, she'd suck the end of her pen. Then, she'd pass a note or a letter over my shoulder. Sometimes, she'd ring Richard Kay, the

Daily Mail journalist and a trusted friend, for his opinion. He was her expert wordsmith and she called him 'Ricardo'.

I would sit with the princess for fifteen to twenty minutes: which was consistent with her short attention span, her hurried lifestyle. Then she would dart back up the stairs, and I would return to the pantry.

The walls of the hall, vestibule and staircase were not always yellow. In fact, they were only that colour for the last year of the princess's life. Yellow had replaced peach, which had dominated since the Prince and Princess of Wales had taken charge of Apartments 8 and 9 after their wedding in 1981. With divorce imminent at the end of summer 1996, the boss had wanted to place her own individual stamp on KP. She wanted her home to reflect her tastes, not Prince Charles's.

It is not true, as other observers have suggested, that she expunged all memories and remnants of the prince from those apartments—although I saw her put a collection of china that bore the Prince of Wales feathers into a bin bag, then smash it with a hammer. It was her way of dealing with anger, she said. Later, she had sessions with a kick-boxer— the cheaper alternative, I joked! However, she kept framed photographs of Prince Charles, as a loving father, in her sitting room and bedroom. He took from KP some treasured possessions, but also a pair of upholstered Georgian chairs *circa* 1780 from the drawing room. The boss described them as 'hideous chairs', which was probably why they were pushed to one side. One day she said, 'You'll never guess what he wants now! Those portraits of his ancestors!' She pointed to two paintings of

15

Hanoverian forebears that hung against the yellow silk panels in the drawing room. They were duly dispatched to St James's Palace, but one request wasn't granted. Prince Charles had wanted the John Ward watercolours from the staircase. The boss decided that those images of her wedding and the boys' christenings would stay at KP.

When the division of possessions had been finalized, the boss concentrated on a new interior, drawing up plans with her favoured interior designer and friend, Dudley Poplak.

'Let's freshen this place up a little,' he said.

'Make a list of everything we need,' she suggested, 'and let's spend a bit more of *his* money while we can!'

'His money' referred to the budget of her soon-to-be ex-husband. After the divorce, the tab for domestic alterations and household goods would have to be picked up by the boss, not by the Prince of Wales's office. She undertook wholesale change on every front. We bought new towels, sheets, duvet covers, pillowcases, china, crockery, silver and kitchenware.

We walked round KP with a check-list. 'Do we need a new washing-machine?' she asked. I nodded. 'And what about a new dishwasher, microwave and kettle?' she smiled mischievously. I agreed. We decided to throw in a new juicer for the hell of it.

The princess had suddenly started to become more careful with her money, and sought independent financial advice. From the moment she had to stand on her own two feet, she watched the pennies. Some staff received a payrise but we also noticed cut-backs, even down to the number

16

of window-boxes at KP. One memo she sent read: 'It is now not possible to have 5 window boxes outside the dining room and drawing room, please can you remove them and put the surviving plants in the boxes outside the sitting room . . .' She loved flowers, but they were an extravagance—unless, of course, they were a gift from an admirer or friend.

She even drew up a list of nine restaurants that were within her budget: 'The only ones where I shall dine from now on,' she said. It makes me laugh when I think of it now: the princess was attempting to be thrifty but her chosen restaurants were: Caviar Kaspia, Bebendum, Le Caprice, Thomas Goode, Turner's, Cecconi's, the Ritz, Claridges and the Ivy.

At KP, Dudley Poplak drew up designs to transform her favourite rooms from pink, peach and cream to something he described as 'a little more professional and mature': cream, gold and blue. The carpet in the main hall, up the stairs and across the landings was in lime green and orange diamond pattern, embroidered with the Prince of Wales feathers. 'It has to go,' said the boss, and settled on beige-brown with a subtle design. Unfortunately, the silk-embossed hanging panels that covered the walls (they don't use wallpaper in royal residences) was deemed too expensive to replace. So the blue and pink pattern in the sitting room stayed, as did the peach paint in the dressing room. But the princess put yellow and gold in the drawing room and her bedroom. The dining room remained crimson.

The last room to be refurbished was the one where she spent most of her time: the sitting room. The furniture was reupholstered: a candy-striped

17

sofa became a calmer cream; the chairs blue, and a new, long, cream stool on cabriole legs arrived to stand on the massive Aztec-style rug in pink and blue. Pastel blue curtains, with matching pelmets, were hung at the sash windows. All of this took place in mid-August 1997 when she was on the *Jonikal* yacht with Dodi Al Fayed. Sadly, she only ever saw the sitting room's new look once, when she made a fleeting visit to KP on 21 August. Before she dashed off to Stansted Airport and a flight to Nice. There, she was reunited with Dodi to cruise round the French Riviera and Sardinia. I don't know how much pleasure she took in the new colours because on the day she returned to replenish her luggage I wasn't there. I was on holiday with my family in the Republic of Ireland, unaware that I'd never see the boss alive again.

*   *   *

She didn't always wait in the sitting room for me to answer a telephone summons. Frequently, I'd be half-way up the stairs when I'd glance up to find her leaning over the banister, waiting for me, her shoulders hunched round her neck. We'd walk to her desk as she unloaded a thought or asked me to do something. If she was seeking a male opinion on what not to wear, she'd stand on those 'catwalk stairs' and ask, 'What do you think?' then strike a pose. 'With these?' she'd say, flashing a bejewelled earlobe with a dangling earring, and then she'd turn her head to show the other lobe with a diamond stud: 'Or these?' Or one foot would be placed in front of the other. 'With heels? Or without?' 'With stockings? Or without?' Had there

18

been ten staff in the house, she'd have asked each one for their opinion. As it was, she depended on either her dresser or me.

At the top of the stairs and straight ahead was the door to William and Harry's sitting room. It had been Prince Charles's until it was turned into a play den—that room was used for the boss's BBC *Panorama* interview with Martin Bashir in 1995. It was untouched during the refurbishment because the boss understood the importance to her sons of not interfering with their father's tastes and influence. The room for the men remained stuck in its 1981 time-warp, and looked as dated as the television that rested on a mahogany cabinet until a Harrods-donated, wide-screen plasma Sony model arrived in 1997. Both sets provided the boys with endless hours of fun and entertainment: either they were engrossed in their collection of action movies—James Bond, *Lethal Weapon*, *Robocop*, *The Terminator*, *Mission Impossible*—or they spent hours engaged in combat on their Sega Mega Drive, Super Nintendo or PlayStation consoles, always at full volume.

When I was sitting in my pantry, I'd often hear an explosion of noise and knew what would come next because I'd seen or heard whatever game it was so often before.

'Do you think you've got that loud enough, boys?' the princess would shout. Two pairs of sheepish eyes would turn to her, and the volume would suddenly dip.

My sons, Alexander and Nick, were often invited up to the palace to play with William and Harry. As a treat, I would fetch a plateful of Harry's favourite chocolate biscuits: Penguins. Sometimes the princess joined the boys in that room for burgers and fries, fish fingers or spaghetti Bolognese, served on trays or fold-away tables as she sat on a chair against a cushion embroidered with: 'Don't bug me, hug me.'

There were unforgettable times at weekends, during hot London summers, when the princess and her boys came down to where we lived at the Old Barracks to play rounders on the green that stretched out in front of our home. As a family, we'd spot the princess, in a flowing skirt and short sleeves, on her bicycle, complete with basket at the front, coasting down the drive that runs past the staff living quarters, connecting the palace to Kensington High Street. At either side of her, pedalling furiously to keep up on their BMX bikes, were the two princes, in shorts and T-shirts.

I'll never forget how determined the boss was to win, especially at rounders. She wanted to win at *everything*. I'd always be captain yet everyone wanted to be on the 'princess's team'. She'd be giggling even before it was her turn to bat, and would laugh as she belted the ball, then ran from base to base, feet bare on the grass. She cheered, clapped and jumped up and down with the rest of us.

*   *   *

At the top of the stairs and down a short landing, another four paces would take you to the drawing-room door, on the left and, straight ahead, the door to the boss's sitting room. The balustrade that looked over the stairwell was on the right-hand side. The drawing room was where I took guests to wait before the princess received them. It was where she conducted formal entertaining, receptions, business meetings, pre-lunch drinks and chats. An eighteenth-century Flemish tapestry seized the eye as it took up an entire wall, from cornice to dado-rail, and spread at least twenty feet wide. It was the backdrop for a long cream and gold silk-upholstered couch—which looked so delicate that I can't remember a single guest sitting on it. Most visitors tended to stand with a drink in hand as they nervously anticipated the arrival of the boss. Flanking that couch, and positioned at right angles to it, were two peach-upholstered armchairs with tassel-fringed skirts to the carpet and two end-tables beside each that bore framed photos on piles of books, stacked four or five high. That was typical of the boss—she placed a photo wherever she found a flat surface. One of her favourite images of herself with her boys stood on one such pile—the black-and-white head shot of Harry, Mum and William, taken by Patrick Demarchelier. One year she used it inside the Christmas cards she sent to friends and family.

On the other side of the room was a fireplace, its marble surround standing five feet high. In front of it, facing each other, two lime-green sofas were scattered with peach and yellow cushions. I remember two ladies, smartly dressed in suits, kneeling on the carpet between these sofas poring over papers, sheets and charts spread out before them. The princess was 'in session' with her favourite and most-trusted adviser, Debbie Frank, in June 1997. Intricate diagrams of the universe and the planets spilled across the carpet, and the boss—a Cancerian whose birthday was on 1 July—

was enthralled by everything Debbie said. The astrologer became a good friend, one of the few who wasn't dropped for being too familiar or 'wacko'. The boss adored her. Even when Debbie was asked to analyse the charts of Charles and Camilla, she was brave enough, and respected enough, to tell the boss the harsh truth: that they were 'well matched'. When Debbie came to lunch, the boss always had a private reading, and the intensity of those sessions was always in sharp contrast to the girlish banter and gossip at the dining table.

I remember the drawing room as a place for formal discussions, friendly chatter, the clink of crystal champagne glasses—and the boss bounding in to meet a guest, smiling, arms wide. I'm sure many visitors, formal or otherwise, have fond memories of that room. But, for me, it was also a room that was filled with music. Her Steinway grand piano was positioned between two Georgian sash windows, each topped with a ruched, peach pelmet. It was there that I often caught her playing the few bars of Rachmaninov's Piano Concerto No. 2 that she had mastered, head back, eyes closed. She would sit there at quiet times by herself over the weekend, or in the evenings after a busy day, when the work at her desk was done. It was one way she chose to unwind.

On one particular day, she didn't quite unwind. She was more in a spin, continually revolving on the spot. Two men and a woman had arrived at the front door with trunks, instruments and briefcases. I showed them in to the drawing room where I had already moved back the sofas, leaving a vast open space on the carpet. They set up their equipment, which included a metal-plated, revolving turntable. Meanwhile, the princess was in her dressing room, squeezing into a skin-tight leotard as the guests had requested. They needed to take 'precise' measurements. It was 1997 and they had come from Madame Tussaud's waxworks museum in London.

The boss greeted the trio with a smile. 'Hello, everybody!' she said, and they got down to the business in hand. The princess was asked to stand on the metal plate in the centre of the room. Suddenly, she looked like a doll in a musical box, and was overcome by a fit of giggles. 'I'm afraid we must ask you to stand still,' someone said meekly, and the boss—eventually—composed herself. Giant callipers and tape measures were produced. Cameras flashed. Every inch of her anatomy, every curve, had to be measured exactly, from the width of her head to the width of her hips; the length of her nose (always a sore point with the princess) to that of her inside leg. It took around two hours, and she stepped down twice to take a break. I was back and forth with tea, coffee, and sandwiches, and water for the boss.

For me, history was repeating itself. In my days as footman to Her Majesty the Queen, I had accompanied the Queen, and her corgis, to the Chinese Drawing Room at Buckingham Palace for the official inspection of the finished product.

Sadly, the boss never saw *her* finished product, but the figure that stands today in Madame Tussaud's is a superb representation of her.

The drawing room was between the dining room and the sitting room. A connecting door—adjacent to the windows—led to the all-crimson dining

23

room, where the colour smacked guests between the eyes when they walked in. A round table, draped in white linen that fell to the carpet, stood in the centre of the room surrounded by latticed bamboo chairs, with red upholstered seats. A crystal chandelier with candle lights hung above, and a sideboard, again draped in linen, was pushed against one wall. In the mornings an electric toaster and a hot-plate for the Herend china coffee pot stood on it. Her breakfast comprised a slice of wholemeal toast, half a grapefruit, a spoonful of honey, and black coffee, no sugar. She'd sit at the table in her white towelling robe, scanning the morning's papers, sometimes with a towel wrapped turban-style round wet hair. Each morning, the boss ran herself a bath—she never took showers—and appeared for breakfast around eight.

Lunch was formal or relaxed, depending on the company. If it was someone like Debbie Frank, the boss's barriers were down. If it was Paul Dacre, editor of the *Daily Mail,* they were up and fortified behind a charming façade. Lunch with Raine Spencer, her stepmother, sticks in my mind—because I didn't always get things right at KP. Even when I tried to impress. Or, as the princess would say, when I 'tried too hard'. I had wanted the Countess to marvel at my floristry skills. Which she did—at first. As I stood behind the boss, pulling back her chair for her to be seated, her stepmother was all oohs and aahs and 'Isn't that just wonderful?' as she surveyed the arrangement. There were smiles from the boss, and a murmured, 'Well done,' from the corner of the boss's mouth as she sat down, and I left the room. But now the two ladies realized they couldn't see each other. My arrangement, with its foliage spilling over onto the table, was too big. When I returned with the starter, my beautiful display had been relegated to the floor, placed out of the way. 'Beautiful, but far too big.' explained Raine, apologetically. There was a wet patch on the table-cloth where the basket had leaked. The boss saw my disappointment, and folded her lips to stop herself laughing. And then she laid a napkin over the damp linen, and continued chatting to Raine.

The sitting room was relatively small, the heart and soul of the princess's home, where she spent much of her time. She filled the shelves with her favourite things. 'This will all be worth something one day,' she said, as she reached into the open-faced white cabinet against the wall behind her desk, to take down a china rabbit, part of her treasured Herend animal collection, which also included elephants, sea lions, unicorns, pheasants, cockerels and fish. She was for ever re-arranging them and sometimes put them on the mantelpiece.

Queen Mary had collected miniature furniture and possessions for the doll's house now on public display at Windsor Castle, and the princess believed that one day her china collection would be a treasured addition to the Royal Collection. But it never was. Instead it was boxed up—with the Halcyon Days enamel pillboxes that covered a glass-topped end-table—and sent to her ancestral home at Althorp.

Pictures of ballerinas hung on the walls, a reminder of her childhood passion. 'I dreamed of becoming a ballerina,' she said, 'but I was too tall.' She liked to watch the English National Ballet at rehearsal, yearning to be among the dancers, and two pairs of pink satin pointe shoes hung by their ribbons from a hook on the door that led to the landing. In that room, there were signs of her sense of humour. Stickers saying *'I Like Di'* and *'CAUTION: Princess on board'* were plastered on to the marble fireplace. In one corner of the room, between the window and the Herend china collection, hung two of her favourite watercolours in gold frames, one of a kingfisher, which had been a wedding present, the other of William as a cheeky infant, in a blue and white striped jumper. A giant cuddly hippo slumped in front of the desk, between the two sofas where she sat, legs curled beneath her, to watch black-and-white movies, the news, *Brookside, Blind Date, EastEnders* and *Casualty.*

That area in front of the sofas was used for dress-fittings when Jacques Azagury and Catherine Walker visited to oversee operations. The boss would kick off her shoes and stand on a small stool as fitters pinned a hem or took a measurement. 'Isn't it beautiful? Isn't Jacques clever?' I remember her saying once, as she twirled on that stool. Or 'What do you think of this colour?' she'd ask.

She spent an inordinate amount of time at her desk, talking on the telephone, penning an endless stream of thank-you notes, signing official correspondence, writing letters to friends, putting down her thoughts on paper. She kept her vocabulary list propped against a letter rack and used it as a quick reference for words she found hard to spell, such as 'conscientiously' and 'infinitely'. Words, by her own admission, were not her strong point. She'd sit at that desk and write postcards or short notes to William and Harry, sometimes two a day. Frequently they'd say no more than 'Can't wait to hug you!' and she always sent them 'huge kisses and enormous hugs'. A silver ink stand was positioned in front of that list: a three-sided ornamental tray with a crystal pot as an inkwell at its centre, and a grooved channel for her to lay down the black fountain pen she used for all correspondence. A bottle of blue-black Quink was kept to hand near the blue leather blotter—always filled with pink paper, always covered with dark splodges. It was here especially that the boss surrounded herself with William and Harry, in little framed snapshots to right and left on her desk. A tiny, open locket lay on the ink stand, with thumbnail photos of her boys. It had been a gift from the readers of *Woman's Own* magazine, which she flicked through for its real-life stories about women. She had once hosted its annual 'Children of Courage Awards' and the locket had been presented to her as a memento. She treasured it.

When she left for that holiday in August 1997, she had ensured her desk was neat and tidy—she was fastidious in that way. In the hours after her death, I was drawn to the sitting room and the desk, and it struck me how organized everything was. There were three miniature clocks, ticking quietly, a dozen pencils crammed into a beaker, and a miniature marble statue of Jesus Christ, with the rosary beads given to her by Mother Teresa draped round the arms and neck.

It's easy for me to bring to mind the vision of the boss sitting at that carefully arranged desk. Whenever I was in the tiny first-floor pantry that adjoined the dining room, I could see her through all of the open, interconnecting doors. I'd be three rooms away but could always see her at the far end of the palace. And she'd be sitting in that seat, her back against her pink cushion, head down, scribbling away, sometimes looking up to gaze out of the windows as she searched for a phrase or new train of thought.

My two abiding recollections of the boss, imprinted on my memory, are simple ones: of the infectious giggle that could break out anywhere and at any time, and the quiet sight of her at that desk, endlessly writing.

*   *   *

At the top of the stairs a left turn led immediately to a small lobby where there was a cupboard, a passenger lift, its doors disguised as a bookcase, and a door that led up to a narrower staircase to the boys' nursery and bedrooms. Straight on, there was a long corridor with six high windows overlooking a cobbled courtyard with an ornamental well in the centre. Outside, the windows of the boys' sitting room were to the right, and ahead the butler Harold Brown's apartment. (He went eventually to work for Princess Margaret.) To the left lay the apartment of Sir Michael Peat, then the Keeper of the Privy Purse and Treasurer to the Queen.

Every evening the boss went to each window and pulled the string to close the wooden slats of the Venetian blinds. She not only guarded her privacy in public, but protected it, too, from the inside.

That corridor felt claustrophobic because half of its width was taken up with cupboards that stood

28

with their backs to the walls, facing the windows. Once the doors were open, it was impossible to pass through.

The first entrance that came up on the left was covered with a curtain, not a door, and led into her main L-shaped, walk-through wardrobe with one section for daywear, one section for eveningwear; each suit, dress or coat hung on its own padded silk hanger. I walked through that wardrobe to an archway that led into the boss's dressing room, between her bathroom on the left, and her bedroom on the right. This was the inner sanctum few people ever saw.

On many mornings, I delivered a glass of freshly squeezed carrot juice to the princess after breakfast as she sat in her white towelling robe on a bamboo chair, in front of her dressing-table in the window. She'd see me approaching in the oval mirror that stood on the glass top where she kept her hairspray, perfume, makeup, cotton-wool pads and buds, and brushes. She'd reach out, take the glass, and thank me. More often than not, her hair was being blow-dried by stylist Sam McKnight, who also became a confidant—even princesses gossip with their hairdresser! She would sip the carrot juice, reading a letter or the newspaper, as Sam worked on her hair, occasionally shouting to make herself heard above the noise of the hairdryer. 'HAVE YOU SEEN THIS, PAUL? SAM WAS JUST SAYING THAT . . .' and it was quite comical at times as I stood there, straining to hear what she was saying.

The woman I saw on those occasions was not the fashion icon, the royal celebrity or the high-profile humanitarian, but a woman without the mask of royalty and fame. Others might remember her for a dazzling public engagement, when she was wowing crowds in a stunning dress, in her jewels and tiara, every inch the beautiful princess, but I remember her best for being 'Diana' at home, for her being—and for me knowing—the ordinary woman behind-closed-doors. Believe me, it was an immense privilege.

Yet my lasting memory of that dressing room is not of the princess sitting in her robe, but of the wall-to-wall images of William and Harry, which charted their growth from babies to infants to boys. It was a museum to a mother's love for her sons. There were thirteen large framed black-and-white portraits on one wall alone: mother and sons photographed in bales of hay at Highgrove; brothers back to back, cuddling their rabbit and guinea pig; William and Harry embracing their mother, larking about, or rocking with laughter as the photographer captured official poses among off-guard moments. Even in the bathroom there were framed photos of the boys as babies at bathtime.

And the boss arranged her own photographic montage on her dressing-table, inserting snapshots between the glass and the table top, so that she could see them each morning as she did her hair and applied her makeup. There must have been fifteen or so photos under the glass, and she'd refresh the collection from time to time, inserting a new picture that showed a recent milestone reached in her boys' lives. Wherever she walked in KP, there was always an image of her boys to remind her of the good that had come from her marriage to the Prince of Wales.

FRIENDSHIP

Four days after her death, I received a brown envelope from a famous and thoughtful friend of the boss. It contained a cassette-tape—or, rather, it contained her voice.

A handwritten note had been tucked inside the transparent box, which read: 'Dear Paul, Something small to remember your boss—with best wishes and thanks.' It was a copy of an answering-machine message she had left him shortly before her death in the summer of 1997. I knew what it was as soon as I saw the label on the cassette: it read, 'Diana phone message'. 'When the time is right, you should listen to this. It will make you smile,' the friend told me at the time.

In the horrendous days of that autumn, I toyed with that cassette, turning it over and over in my hands, wanting to play it, wanting to hear her voice but unable to bring myself to press 'play'. There was a funeral to help arrange, a 'home' to keep safe, a legacy to protect, and a million and one other things in accordance with my on-going duty. Then the sound of her voice would have knocked me sideways so I put it away safely. Month by month, year by year, I kept going to that envelope—but could never listen to the tape. To this day, I still struggle when I see moving images or hear her voice on television when she is featured in a documentary. Seeing film footage or hearing her voice was distressing for many years. It was almost as if she was still around and I *wanted* her still to be around, beckoning me again from the top of the stairs. For the best part of a decade, I've walked out of the room or closed my ears when footage of her appears on television.

But in writing this book, I needed to confront that ghost. If this book is about remembrance, and a vivid recall of the woman, then hearing her unique voice had to be part of the process. In the summer of 2006, I went to retrieve the brown envelope from its safe place. Then, when no one else was around, I sat down and listened to the tape for the first time since it had been given to me in September 1997.

I turned the volume to maximum and pressed 'play'. There was the sound of running tape, then the beep of an answering-machine, and her voice, as clear and jolly as ever, as if I was listening to her speaking in the sitting room at KP, from her desk, on the phone. As the tape played, she might have been standing behind me again. I might have been tending a vase of flowers as she went about her normal routine. Of course, books are incapable of relaying sound to a reader but I can at least share the message she left on the friend's phone: it captures her spirit, her carefree nature, her sense of fun and mischief.

Although tears rolled down my face when I heard it, I smiled too. She used to call photographs 'happy snaps', so perhaps this can be seen as a 'happy message'. After the beep to leave a recorded message, she said:

'Hi, it's the elusive Diana here . . . erm . . . I wondered if you'd like to come over next Tuesday, the 20th, about eleven o'clock—if you're out of your bed by then!—for a cup of herbal tea, and Paul says we can spice it up with some marijuana if

32

that . . . erm . . . excites you into a frenzy! We hope to see you then. Sorry I missed your call, hope you're okay . . . lots of love, bye-bye.'

I knew instantly why my friend had said it was 'something small to remember your boss'. The message only lasted about thirty seconds but her light-hearted tone, the mischievous mention of marijuana, the joke we had shared that day, before she left that message, brought back a simple memory. It was the joke about being out of bed by eleven o'clock, the ever-so-polite invitation for a herbal tea, the apology for missing a call, the warmth and friendliness in that briefest of messages. And the way she said, 'We hope to see you then,' always 'we', princess and butler, welcoming visitors and friends. That afternoon, I must have played it over and over again more than twenty times; when I had familiarized myself once more with the sound of her voice, it became a comfort—a friend instead of a ghost from the past.

I'm not sure that I ever thanked that friend for his kindness and consideration in giving me the tape. I was not brave enough to appreciate its worth until almost a decade later, but it was a simple act of friendship that I'll never forget. And it was friendship—with simple gestures of kindness—that made the boss's world go around.

*   *   *

She spent an incalculable amount of time thinking about how she could put a smile on friends' faces, whether it was a quick message on an answering-machine, a letter, a small gift or an invitation to lunch or dinner. Whether she was penning a note

33

or ordering a bouquet of flowers, a birthday cake or a bottle of champagne, the 'giving' nature of the boss was part of her magic. It amazed me how much time she invested in friends, regardless of her schedule, regardless of the rush, rush, rush of her life, but it showed how crucial a role they played in her life—more important to her than her family, with the exceptions of William and Harry. Friends *were* her preferred family. And it is the memories of friendship, fun and laughter that bring a smile to my face.

Tuesday night was music night at KP, and the princess always looked forward to these weekly occasions. She would run through the front door, skip up the stairs and ask: 'Is Maureen here yet?' I'd hear the voice before I saw her.

Maureen Stevens was a clerk from the Prince of Wales's office at St James's Palace, the *only* person from 'the other camp' allowed anywhere near Apartments 8 and 9. Ordinarily, it would have been unthinkable for anyone in Prince Charles's world to enter them but Maureen was trusted and respected. More importantly, KP wouldn't have been the same without her musical talents. Because Maureen, the epitome of a clerk with her handbag and gloves, row of pearls and clipped eloquence, was a classically trained pianist, and arrived each Tuesday to provide the princess with a private piano recital. It became a highlight of the week. Anyone who knew the princess will remember that she adored the piano, so Maureen would play the Steinway grand. I can visualise it as if it were yesterday: Maureen perched on the stool, her sheets of music stacked on top of the piano— just finding enough room among the leather-framed family portraits, mainly of the boss, William and Harry—as her fingers danced over the keys. As the music filled her home, the princess would sit at her desk in the adjoining sitting room, continuing with her work or correspondence. I don't think Maureen ever tired of providing such joy for the boss, and the boss never tired of Maureen, occasionally drifting into the drawing room to tell her how much she had enjoyed a particular piece. Maureen would nod and smile, then continue to play tunes from the *King and I*, *The Sound of Music*, *South Pacific* or the princess's favourites: 'A Nightingale Sang in Berkeley Square' or Rachmaninov's Piano Concerto No. 2. They were fun times, which put a spring in my step as I went about my duties, answering the telephone or preparing the princess's trolley for her dinner, timed for when Maureen had left.

The princess never minded me walking around, singing. She said it filled the apartment with life. 'I hate the silence of this home,' she said once, while she was flicking through a magazine on a Saturday morning. In the summer months, when the windows were wide open, Princess Michael of Kent, who lived next door, would hear Maureen playing and once remarked to the princess, 'I thoroughly enjoyed last night's performance. Thank you.'

Sometimes one of the princess's close friends, the late Dr Mary Loveday, would be with her in her sitting room on Tuesday nights. 'I love that experience, Paul,' she'd say, as she walked to the door. 'It's such fun here. You're so lucky!'

Other friends noticed how relaxed life was at KP. One afternoon the journalist Richard Kay was with the boss in the sitting room watching a documentary about her. With my duties done, I joined them and sat back against the sofa. Then some archive footage popped up on the screen from my days as footman to the Queen. Both the boss and Richard started teasing me about the 'panto-style' uniform and the boss glanced at my legs. 'I never knew you had *such* nice calves!' she said, and collapsed into giggles. There was no room for pomp, ceremony or liveried uniforms at KP.

Pictures of friends were dotted round the apartments. One that springs to my mind stood on the piano and was referred to as 'the three black crows'. It featured the boss's strongest and most enduring friendship. It was a picture of her with Lucia Flecha de Lima, the wife of the then Brazilian ambassador. 'I couldn't cope without her. She's like a mother to me,' said the boss. And she was: she was always there for her day or night, on the telephone no matter where she was in the world.

The photograph shows the princess standing between Lucia and her daughter, with a seven-foot-high hedge behind them; all three women are dressed in black. She would point it out to friends when they came to lunch at KP: 'Have you seen that picture? We're the three black crows!' Then she would proudly show off a photo of her being embraced by Luciano Pavarotti.

Lucia represented the essence of what was required—or, rather, expected—in a friend: being on call 24 hours a day, seven days a week, able to drop what she was doing and respond in a flash when advice was sought or a favour needed doing.

To be a friend to the princess could be emotionally exhausting, and it was not for the faint-hearted or those short on patience. But the inner circle, which included Rosa Monckton, Susie Kassem, Lady Annabel Goldsmith, Lana Marks, Richard Kay and, until relations soured, Sarah, Duchess of York, understood all of that. They saw the princess at her most raw and accepted her with all her faults and flaws. She was only human, after all, and could be as difficult as the next person.

'I'm trouble with a capital T, but I never forget my friends,' she said to me one day.

If she regarded you as a friend, she stuck by you and protected you, and her warmth and generosity were worth everything. She embraced each friend who came through the doors at KP or when they met at a restaurant. I can see her now in the KP sitting room, perched on the edge of the sofa, eagerly listening to what a friend had to say.

Her friends came from all walks of life, each chosen with care, each made to feel special. Ironically, it was only after the princess's death that all those friends met for the first time; from the inner circle of her 'surrogate family' to the more peripheral figures and associates; it was the first time that mother-figure Lucia met sister-figures Susie Kassem and Rosa Monckton. I looked around Westminster Abbey on the day of her funeral, 6 September 1997, and realized it was the only time that those friends had gathered under the same roof. Indeed, it was the only time the princess would have *permitted* them to be united: in life, she had kept them deliberately apart. She jealously guarded the individuality of each bond, and had the knack of making someone feel they were her most indispensable friend. There were no girls' nights in or out, no dinner parties at which like-minded friends would gather for a gossip. She compartmentalized them, sorting them into boxes, and I knew which box she was opening, the significance of what it contained, and where it ranked in her life. I was at the centre of her world, with permission to look through her address book to find a name, a number and set up an appointment, so I had an overview of the entire jigsaw.

As Rosa Monckton said, in an article published in the *Sunday Telegraph* on 3 November 2002: 'Diana chose to live her life in compartments . . . Only Paul had the key to all the doors.'

On the day of her funeral all those doors were flung open: each person was able to share stories and anecdotes and a secret club was free to discuss openly its memories of the chairman. Westminster Abbey was packed with the people who had had a connection with the princess, but only a select few had belonged to her inner sanctum and shared with me an intimate knowledge of a royal world. They were a group who had provided the boss with more love and support than the Spencers or Windsors ever could.

The princess only allowed a handful of friends to get truly close to her. I suspect one of the main reasons that other friends were discarded was that she feared their becoming too close. I believe that the distance she put between herself and those she 'froze out', or the friends she did not regard as part of the inner circle, can be explained by her understanding of her own behaviour. The princess was a great one for wanting to find herself, to understand herself better.

One day, at her desk, she posted a philosophy she had written out in her own hand, and I think it now serves as a partial explanation for the fences she put up around her. I don't know where it came from but it said: 'Greatest barrier to bonding is low self-esteem itself. A woman with low self-esteem may choose to live without much intimacy. She might be terrified of letting someone get too close lest they discover the 'real' her & reject.' So, I think the princess cut loose certain people before they could let her down. She almost craved the devotion of those who were 'allowed in', and knowing how to say the right thing and not overstep the mark became a skill in itself. If anyone abused their closeness with an opinion that might have been a little too candid, then the princess would drop them like a stone. Friendship was expected to be unconditional and non-judgmental.

The sadness of being a friend to the princess was that we could not rid her of private unhappiness. There was the image of the princess—the image the public adored and the media chased—and then there was the real princess who, behind closed doors, had terrible bouts of misery. She was an actress who played a role on the public stage, then retired to her dressing room and wondered where her real life had gone. Global popularity and celebrity did not bring happiness. Understandably, the princess leaned on her friends because that is what friends are for. She needed them, at all hours and on all occasions, to be there. One of the many philosophies she recited was about true friendship: 'The worst solitude is to be destitute of sincere friendship.' Thankfully, she had a coterie of sincere friends who never allowed her to be lonely, and were always on hand. In return, the reward was *her* friendship. We became beneficiaries of one of the warmest, kindest and most generous spirits of all.

*   *   *

I can see her now, standing in front of the mahogany wardrobe on the first floor, a storage area next to the lift, tucked away at the top of the main staircase. The doors of the wardrobe were open and the princess, her back to me, was looking up at the shelves which were stacked high with gifts: scented candles, Hermès ties, toys, Chanel handbags, perfume, costume jewellery, all collected throughout the year. It was a scene played out every Christmas: the princess would spend hours thinking about the gifts she wanted to send.

'I think Susie would like this,' she would say, standing on tiptoe to make a choice. 'And this would be ideal for Rosa.' The selection process was under way. She stood there with a bundle of Post-its and a pen. When she had pinpointed a gift, she'd scribble a name, stick it to the packaging, and hand it to me for wrapping. I'd then place it on the floor by the skirting-board. By the end, there must have been more than a hundred gifts, tagged with yellow Post-its. It looked like a factory production line. The princess was one of those people who enjoyed giving presents much more than she did receiving them. And her generosity, as I knew all too well, could be overwhelming.

Others benefited from the boss's generosity. Aromatherapist Eileen Malone, mother of the cosmetics entrepreneur Jo Malone, was sent an ornate carriage clock, *Washington Post* publisher Katharine Graham received a silver box from Asprey with 'K' inscribed on the lid, and Christie's expert Meredith Etherington-Smith was sent a specially-made gold starfish brooch scattered with diamonds and inscribed on the reverse: 'With fondest love from Diana'.

One gift the world never learned about was commissioned for a man in London. The time and trouble she took in arranging it and ensuring it was perfect said much about her fondness for this debonair individual. It was a custom-made, silver-gilt, watercolour paintbox with an engraving of a frog on a lilypad painting a princess. It was the most exquisite piece I had ever seen, and cost in the region of £20,000. The princess wanted to see the look on the recipient's face when he unwrapped it and made sure she delivered it in person. It made her day when she saw his eyes light up. It would be a mistake to assume it was a gift for Prince Charles, who loves watercolours. Nor was it for James Hewitt or Dodi Al Fayed. The identity of the recipient is not relevant. The story illustrates, along with the many others, how the princess gave 110 per cent, and went out of her way to make certain people feel extra special.

Loyalty was also rewarded, as I discovered after I became butler at KP in April 1993. She gave my family, and other servants, much over the years as a thank-you for the long hours she demanded of her staff. Among the many items and trinkets she gave to us was a writing bureau, presented to the

Prince and Princess of Wales by the city of Aberdeen to mark their wedding in 1981, so that my son Alexander had somewhere to do his homework; a Cartier clock, because she thought it was 'hideous'; and a host of other ornaments. She gave hats, shoes and dresses to my wife Maria, shirts, ties, gold pens, watches and cufflinks to me.

It was this generosity that ultimately brought Scotland Yard to my doorstep in 2001, when detectives discovered a 'treasure trove' of items of royal provenance; it sent me to trial at the Old Bailey in London, charged with stealing 315 items from the estate of Diana, Princess of Wales. I was acquitted, and the outside world learned that for centuries royalty had handed things on to their staff, servants and friends. 'No one understands how much the princess gave, how much she shared. No one understands her world, and it's a travesty of the truth and her memory,' I remember telling my lawyers shortly before the case collapsed in November 2002.

The irony of the trial was that the princess's mother, Mrs Frances Shand Kydd, who has since died, knew little about her daughter's generous nature. She asserted in her testimony: 'She was very, very careful with all things royal . . . I can promise you, she gave nothing away other than gifts she usually bought for Christmas and birthdays.'

As I've said, her friends were the family who knew the princess best, and statements such as that one, from her mother, prove the point for me.

It was Francis Bacon who said, 'Who can I tear to pieces, if not my friends? If they were not my friends, I could not do such violence to them.'

There are probably some friends of the princess who might have easily attributed those words to her because she was as maddening as she was lovable. As with all friendships, there were downsides and bad times. Friendship is supposed to weather that.

Her brother, the Earl Spencer, criticized his sister in a letter—in April 1996—that reduced her to tears: 'I view the consternation and hurt your fickle friendship has caused so many . . .'

It is the view of a brother who neither knew properly nor understood his sister; he was lashing out at having become 'a peripheral part of your life', as he described it. He wasn't the first to feel isolated by the princess.

I, too, had witnessed 'the consternation and hurt' the princess had caused others. And I sensed when ill-feeling was in the air. I'd know by the arrivals and departures at KP what mood surrounded a certain friendship. If the princess was waiting for a visitor in her sitting room, heard the doorbell ring or the crunch of gravel outside, then bounded down the stairs to meet them, it meant that this friend was as close as they could possibly be. But if the princess remained in the sitting room, preoccupied with a telephone call or other business, and the visitor was made to wait before going in to see her—that was a different matter. In those instances, everything seemed matter-of-fact, and the meetings were uneasy, for whatever underlying reason. I watched them all come and go, the joyful and the sad.

I remember Dr Mary Loveday leaving in floods of tears one evening after a six-thirty appointment. She was the most inoffensive, kind and gentle lady whom the princess adored and had told many times how much she appreciated her advice as well as the homeopathic treatments she offered. Mary's mistake was to take the boss's 'appreciation of your advice' as *carte blanche* to become a little too open and candid in her views. One day, she said too much—at least, she said too much in the eyes of the boss. From the warm glow of being in favour, Mary was suddenly at the end of an icy blast. She was asked to leave. I caught her coming down the stairs, and she was visibly shocked. We went into the equerry's room at the foot of the main staircase, and I consoled her. I told her what a difficult week the princess had been having and how fragile she was at the moment, advising her to tread carefully. It would blow over soon and be forgotten. 'Don't take it to heart. The princess doesn't mean to be hurtful,' I reassured her. As we walked out of the room, the princess was standing on the stairs. My heart raced, then sank. She had crept half-way down the stairs and heard every word. The moment our eyes met, I knew I was in trouble.

I had been attempting to help Dr Loveday, attempting to be the diplomat, but the princess would never understand that. As far as she was concerned, and she made this clear, I had been talking about her behind her back. She didn't speak to me for three days, but I didn't take it to heart and, yes, it soon blew over. To know the princess was to know how to handle her, when to say something, and when to keep quiet.

That day, I learned a valuable lesson in minding my own business and letting matters outside my control take their own course. I had to stand back and say nothing when the princess became hot-headed over a planned trip to Greece with another female friend. We were standing in the sitting room, and the departure for a flight to Athens had been brought forward, sending the princess into a tailspin. She was *always* in a rush so this instantly made matters worse. The friend could not have known of the sudden change in the schedule and hadn't even set off for the palace from her home in west London. But the princess rang her, wanting to know where she was. 'We're going to be late if you don't hurry up and get here!'

Ten minutes later, when the princess was ready, she started to pace the floor. 'Where is she? Where is she?' she kept saying, as this friend was no doubt breaking all records, as well as blood vessels, to make it across to Kensington.

I was helpless to do anything, so I stood motionless as the princess panicked. Time ran out. She rang the friend on her mobile as she dashed downstairs: 'I couldn't wait a moment longer for you!' That was it. She was out of the door and on her way to the airport alone.

Fifteen minutes later, the friend arrived at the door, breathless, with tears in her eyes. She was distraught, convinced that she actually had let down the boss. I consoled her, made her a cup of tea and tried to explain. It was a mark of this wonderful woman, and what an especially tolerant friend she was to the princess, that she shelved her anger and attempted to understand the exceptional circumstances. She forgave the princess and, because true friendship was unconditional, continued to be there, offering love and support. With such unstinting friendship

45

around her, it's fair to say that the princess might have regarded herself as the lucky one.

* * *

If there was one thing the princess couldn't abide, it was not being told the truth. It came down to trust, and even a small white lie could shake hers. If anyone dared tap-dance their way round the truth with the boss, it spelled the beginning of the end of an association, whether personal or professional. Just ask her dresser, Helen Walsh, and her chauffeur, Steve Davies.

The princess had long suspected that those two members of staff had grown close and, in her mind, that was risky in itself. It meant there was a danger of two separate compartments merging. For a woman who kept staff, as well as friends, compartmentalized, this could not be allowed to happen. Helen knew the goings-on behind closed doors while Steve didn't. Steve knew about the travel plans and destinations and Helen didn't. The mere prospect of that information being intimately shared—even though, in all likelihood, it wasn't—exercised the princess.

Until then, Helen could not have been more in favour. Like my wife Maria, she had been given unwanted clothes, handbags and shoes as a thank-you for her loyalty and service. So, the princess expected honesty from her dresser.

'I've had enough,' said an exasperated princess, 'Come with me, I want you to witness this.'

It was early one evening, just before dinner, and no force could have stopped her as she hurried down the stairs and out of the front door.

This was a princess on a mission. She marched across the gravel, with me trying to keep up, and we headed for Nottingham Cottage, home of Princess Margaret's private secretary, and the Upper Stables, staff accommodation.

'Stay behind that wall,' she told me, pointing to a red-brick pillar at the end of the walled garden, and then she went on towards the staff accommodation. 'And I want you to listen!' she shouted back to me as she marched on, arms pumping. It would have been comical, had her mood been less thunderous.

The pillar, my hiding-place, was in full view of Helen's front door on the ground floor at the end of the cobbled courtyard, and I felt a bit silly. But I stood there, as I had been told, watching and listening. I was being dragged into a domestic fracas that, in the boss's mind, had been brewing for some time.

The princess rang the doorbell, keeping it depressed for longer than was necessary. It took Helen a while to answer. When she came to the door, she took a step back with shock. The last person she had expected to find on the doorstep was her boss, Diana, Princess of Wales. 'I *know* he's in here!' said the boss, 'and I will not allow it!'

'I don't know who you're talking about, Your Royal Highness,' Helen said, polite, courteous and respectful as ever. The denial that Steve Davies was tucked away inside her quarters was suspect, as far as the princess was concerned. 'I *will not* allow it, Helen,' the princess repeated, and with that she turned on her heel, having made Helen aware that she *knew*. What Helen could not have known was that the princess had been standing at

47

her drawing-room window minutes earlier and had watched Steve arrive. Heaven knows what Helen, a lovely, down-to-earth woman, must have thought when she saw the princess blazing a trail back to her apartments, with me emerging from behind the pillar, all sheepish and awkward.

Of course, it was none of the princess's business what staff did in their private time but she couldn't stand the thought of her chauffeur and her dresser swapping gossip and stories about her. She had to seize control and stamp it out. After a period of icy relations between dresser and princess, Helen left.

*   *   *

The princess had a wicked sense of humour. If one image is set in my mind it is the sight of her laughing; she had an unstoppable, infectious giggle that bent her double.

Her humour could be risqué, and nothing amused her more than a crude greetings card. She had a large wicker basket in her sitting room, beside her desk, which she filled with cards for all occasions. If there was a Winnie the Pooh card, it was nearly always intended for William or Harry— Winnie the Pooh splashing about in the rain, or Piglet looking forlorn. But for her friends the 'birthday' collection was the source of much fun. 'Look at this! Have you seen this one?' she'd say, when we nipped out to WH Smith in Kensington High Street. She'd read the front, then the inside, open her mouth in mock horror, then laugh, throwing her head back in delight. More often than not, she'd buy a card that poked fun at the Royal Family or the Prime Minister. For female friends, she'd never hesitate to buy a card depicting a bare-chested hunk of a man. For male friends, there would be a titillating image of a scantily clad woman with a teasing message inside.

She was also a practical joker, and so even got a thrill out of the mere purchase of a whoopee cushion. The fact that the Princess of Wales was buying such an item was enough to send her into a fit of giggles. And heaven forbid if anyone happened to break wind or burp in her company—*that* sent her into snorting hysterics, and she became the naughty, mischievous girl that she had once been. She knew how to laugh, and the sound of laughter often filled KP. The princess said frequently that the British people could never know how many tears she had shed over the years, and the heartache she had faced, but those same people, reading of her misery in her marriage, could never know how much laughter there was too.

*   *   *

I have grown used to the media cynicism surrounding my role in the princess's life, to the sniping of newspaper columnists, royal pundits and peripheral associates who would prefer to believe that in her eyes my role was only ever professional. It never ceases to amaze me how those who were never there, and never truly knew the princess, feel able to speak so authoritatively about her, desperate to reshape and warp the truth. Thankfully, the behind-the-scenes truth—supported by her own hand, by her private letters to me—is something no one can either dispute or

49

take away from me. I knew how it felt to be touched by that hand of friendship, and my memories, that knowledge and those letters have comforted me over the years and coated me with a skin thick enough to take all the pot shots aimed at me. I always knew my place with the boss, and never forgot it. First and foremost, I was a reliable employee. In fact, right up until the end, I called her 'Your Royal Highness', even when she had been stripped of that status following her divorce. She was always HRH in my eyes, and those of millions the world over. So, I was a servant on her payroll, yes, but one she *chose* to take with her to KP from Highgrove, which was where a working relationship began to merge into a less formal association. I'm not the first, and neither will I be the last, employee to find themselves on friendly terms with the boss.

At KP, as her reliance on me increased, I found myself invited into a privileged circle of trusted friends and confidants. I will never forget the times we sat and talked in the sitting room, on the stairs, at the breakfast table, in my pantry, in the car and, when she was away, on the telephone. Discussions of schedules and duties would drift into a serious conversation, a moment of friendly advice or some juicy gossip. 'Dramas galore during the past two weeks, and you'd be impressed by these ones! It's wonderful to know you've returned,' she said in one letter she wrote to me after I had returned from a family break in Kentucky.

I never heard her refer to me as 'my rock'. It was friends who told me about that, and the media picked up on it. What she did call me, in personal letters, was 'the captain of my ship', 'my third eye', and she thanked me for being 'such a tower of strength'. 'You are marvellous how you cope with my questions day after day and it's quite annoying that you're constantly right! But, on a serious note, your support, as always, has been invaluable and kept me sane during some of the nightmare times ...' she wrote, in her final letter to me, in 1997.

Whenever the doubters, the jealous or the media pipe up, I tend not to hear them. Instead I read the words of the only person whose views matter: the boss.

She extended her warmth and generosity to the people around me too: Maria, our boys, their nanny, my father, my brother, my friends. When my mum, Beryl, died in 1995, she spent hours comforting my father. When my brother Graham was having marital difficulties, she would ring him at home in Chesterfield to 'talk it all through'. And she would take my boys, Alexander and Nicholas, go-karting with William and Harry.

Even when she departed for Paris on that ill-fated trip in August 1997, she had organized a treat for us Burrells. She had accepted an invitation to attend the Royal Film Premiere of *Hercules*, the new Disney movie, at the Odeon, Leicester Square, in October 1997. Knowing how I loved Disney, and that I collected animation art, she invited me, Maria and our boys to accompany her on that public engagement. What an amazing experience it would have been, to walk up that red carpet with my family behind the princess.

One of my oldest friends, Chuck Webb, was invited to KP to meet the boss, and did his best to fire her interest in all things Disney. He regularly sent her CDs of the latest soundtracks. She adored

51

Elton John's 'Circle of Life' from *The Lion King* and 'A Whole New World' from *Aladdin*. She and I used to sing that one in the car while we were driving through London. Just before her death, she received the *Hercules* soundtrack. Chuck, from Clermont, in Florida, had bought the CD following the film's American release. She played it in the sitting room as soon as it arrived, and then, as she always did when she received a gift, sat down at her desk to compose a thank-you letter. 'If someone has taken the trouble to send me a gift, the least I can do is write them a thank-you letter,' she would say.

Chuck received it, dated 4 June 1997, written on the blue paper she reserved for intimate friends: 'Dear Chuck, I was absolutely thrilled to receive, hot off the press, the 'Hercules' compact disc! Thank you so much for thinking of me, especially as I am going to the opening night of Hercules in October in London. Track 12 is a definite winner! With my best wishes, Diana.'

Track twelve was the Michael Bolton song 'Go The Distance', which struck a chord with the princess, with its lyrics about getting a life back on track, facing the world, being strong and completing a journey, even if it took a lifetime. She played it over and over again, turning it up loud in her sitting room, singing along with the chorus. That letter is now framed in Chuck's house as a treasured keepsake.

Whether it was a letter, a gesture, a gift or a moment of friendship, the boss had an innate ability to make those around her—and even those she contacted occasionally—feel special. But nothing could compare to the extraordinary act of friendship I witnessed in April 1994.

COMPASSION

The sun was shining, and the princess was standing at the window of her sitting room, gazing down at the walled garden, which was coming into blossom, one floor down from Apartments 8 and 9 at KP.

As I walked into the room, she turned. 'Paul, I'd like you to do something for me,' she said. I knew immediately from the words she had used, and her tone, that this was to be an unusual request; when she asked me 'to do something' it usually meant a private mission of a nature apart from normal royal duty. In the past, it had entailed delivering by hand a letter or a message to an address in London or even, once, in New York. There might be a private dinner to arrange or a personal telephone call to make. Sometimes, a visitor was to be smuggled into the palace, lying flat on the back seat of my car under a blanket. Whatever she asked of me, and however outlandish it seemed, it was a duty to be carried out to the best of my ability.

Nothing she had asked of me had either shocked or surprised me—until the request she made on 10 April 1994.

I stood in the middle of the sitting room, facing the desk where she had now sat down. She looked sad but was composed, focused and businesslike. Eventually she described what she would like me to do, and why. That was when the extraordinary nature of the 'duty' almost knocked me off kilter.

Normally, I would take on board her instruction and carry it out. But at that moment I didn't know what to say or think because too many questions about the logistics and practicalities were racing round my mind.

For the first time ever, I voiced my reservation: 'What would the Queen say if she ever found out? I'm concerned that—'

She didn't let me finish. 'Well, Paul, the Queen doesn't need to know,' she said.

'And what should I say if someone sees me?' I persisted.

There was no quick answer to that one. She would think about it, she said, and told me not worry. It was hardly reassuring but the stare she gave me conveyed both her determination, and that she was relying on me.

'Paul, this is something we must do, and I'm asking you to help me,' she said, almost pleading.

At that time, the princess had been sharing more and more of her innermost thoughts and feelings with me, while isolating others. It was a period during which she trusted few, and expected much of me. I didn't fancy falling out of favour by being difficult so I nodded. 'Very well, Your Royal Highness, I understand.'

It was 1994 that the princess began to 'find herself', opening her doors to a band of lifestyle gurus and her mind to new philosophies. It was then that she withdrew—albeit temporarily—from the public spotlight and cancelled all public engagements in protest at the media intrusion in her life, asking for 'time and space' to refocus and take stock after the *Sunday Mirror* had published photographs of her working out at a fitness centre.

54

She made herself available only to her closest friends, and the task she had entrusted to me concerned one of them—Rosa Monckton. That was why it mattered so much. Her decision was final, she said, because she had given Rosa her word.

The execution of this 'duty' would fall to me and her other old-school butler Harold Brown. We would ensure that every detail was correct, and that a delicate situation was handled with extreme sensitivity.

I went downstairs to the pantry and started to make plans for one of the most extraordinary duties of my royal service. Heaven forbid that the grey suits within the Royal Household at Buckingham Palace ever got the faintest sniff of what we were about to do. But the princess had said they had never had hearts so they'd never understand anyway.

I put on my green wellingtons, went outside into the walled garden and grabbed a spade from the shed beside Princess Michael's greenhouse, with my trousers tucked into my wellies, and the sleeves of my white shirt rolled up. The boss was behind me, wearing a navy polka-dot silk dress and her own wellies—she had kicked off her shoes at the front door.

'I think over there, in that corner, Paul,' she said, pointing to a chosen location in the left-hand corner.

I placed my right wellington boot on the top edge of the spade, pressed it down into the soil and began to dig a grave in the royal garden for a baby.

I have thought long and hard about whether to tell this story. But what I witnessed was the ultimate act of compassion and friendship, which I think reflects greatly on the boss and sums up her humanity. Acts of kindness don't get much bigger than this.

The princess had been delighted for Rosa when she had announced the previous autumn that she was expecting her second child, but about six months later, she received terrible news. 'The most awful thing has happened,' she said, eyes red from crying. She explained that Rosa had given birth prematurely to a stillborn baby girl. She kept repeating 'She's lost her baby . . . she's lost her baby,' as if she couldn't take in the enormity of such a loss.

Over the following days, she dropped everything to be with Rosa and Dominic Lawson, her husband. She had arranged with them that the baby would be buried in the walled garden. I don't know why it was chosen as a burial location, perhaps because it was a special place for a special girl, but the couple hadn't known what to do and it had been the princess's idea to bury her in a special place that they could visit whenever they liked. She wanted to help them grieve, and saw no reason why the ceremony couldn't be carried out at KP.

'It's a sanctuary I'm offering them, and a place to help them with their terrible loss,' she said.

My concerns about whether it was appropriate to bury a baby on Crown property were waved aside. By then she had it all figured out and had even worked out what we would say if anyone asked what we were doing. There was a risk that we might be seen from the top police box that overlooked the princess's front door. 'If we're asked, we'll say that these friends of mine are burying a pet. People bury pets in their back gardens all the time,' she said.

It was plausible, but I still wasn't sure. 'Paul, stop worrying,' said the princess, 'We're doing the right thing.'

So it was down to Harold Brown and me to dig the grave in shifts. All other arrangements for a Catholic service had been taken care of, we were told.

The spade work seemed to take all day. I stood with my back to the right angle in the red-brick wall; in a corner sheltered by a tree, which was coming into full blossom. From her sitting-room window, the princess couldn't see the spot because it was shielded from view by the top of the wall, but she knew that the tree marked it. 'It's the nearest point to my window so I'm close enough to watch over it. It's the most appropriate and private place,' she said, as I began to shovel soil into a heap.

'It should be five feet deep,' she said, as my ankles disappeared into the deepening pit.

The princess watched me start, then left me to dig for about an hour. By the time she returned, I was only half-visible, standing in a hole three feet deep.

'Look at you!' she said, wide-eyed, from above me.

My hands were blistered and I was covered with mud. 'Let me help,' she said, and jumped in and took the spade, as I climbed out. She put her back into it, for about ten spades' worth of soil tossed on to the bank—she wanted to do her bit. When she clambered out in her wellies and silk dress, it was

Harold's turn to take the spade until, about two hours later, I returned to finish the job. Between us, the grave had taken six hours to dig.

That evening, the princess examined it with me. She stood in silence, staring into it, lost in her thoughts. When she looked up, her eyes were brimming with tears, but she smiled in the knowledge that everything had gone to plan. In those few quiet moments in the garden, I sensed how important this task was to her.

The following day, 11 April, the burial took place as the mid-afternoon sun cast the wall's shadow over the flower-beds, leaving only the lawn bathed in spring sunshine. Rosa had arranged for a Roman Catholic priest, Father Alexander Sherbrooke, to conduct the simple ceremony. By the time the couple arrived, the boss was waiting for them at the front door, with Harold and me just behind her, in our butler's uniforms: double-breasted navy-blue blazer with gold buttons, white shirt, dark blue trousers and tie. I remember the sombreness and quiet before I heard the car tyres on the gravel. A few moments later, Dominic lifted a little white box out of his hatchback, and cradled it in his arms while the princess went to Rosa. She knew just what to say and do in the most difficult circumstances. She had an innate ability to ease suffering.

However, we did not want to be seen by other people or asked questions at this delicate moment. So priest, princess, butlers, husband and wife hurried across the gravel towards the black wooden door in the wall, which led to the garden. When it swung shut behind us, I think everyone felt more at ease in the privacy afforded by the

58

high walls, and the boss walked slowly with her friend, never letting go of her hand.

Six people gathered around the grave. Harold and I stood at either side, holding two cord straps across it so that we could lower the little coffin into the ground. I remember being in the shade as the sun shone and hearing nothing but the birds chirping. When I glanced at the princess, tears were streaming down her face and she was biting her lip, trying to be strong for the couple: she believed that a dignified ceremony would be an enormous support to them. And it was. I could see how much it meant to Rosa and Dominic as they leaned into each other. Rosa, holding a copy of the Bible and a tiny bunch of flowers, stood between her husband and the princess as the priest said a few words.

Then she spoke in memory of the child she had lost, the daughter she had named Natalia, and read aloud a verse by an Indian poet as Harold and I let the cords slip slowly through our hands, lowering the coffin:

> They who are near me do not know that you
>   are nearer to me than they are.
> They who speak to me do not know that my
>   heart is full with your unspoken words.
> They who crowd in my path do not know that I
>   am walking alone with you.
> They who love me do not known that their love
>   brings you to my heart.

As Rosa's voice trailed away, with the coffin now resting in place, the princess nodded to me—the signal to leave. She and the priest were seconds behind Harold and me, leaving the couple alone to say farewell as the shadows lengthened across the lawn.

The princess had one last thing to do. Earlier that day, she had made sure a key was cut for the garden gate. She had gone out to Kensington High Street in person to get it done. Just before the couple left, the boss pressed the key into Rosa's palm and said: 'This is for you, and you can both come here and visit any time you wish—day or night. It is as much your garden now as it is mine.'

After the couple had left, the princess and I slipped on our wellies again and returned to the garden to fill in the grave. I must have been working too slowly. 'Give me the spade, Paul!' she said, and started to fill it herself. She wanted it over and done with. When the soil had reached the top, we flattened it with our feet.

'Your Royal Highness, what you did today was tremendous,' I said to her. She looked up.

'The only problem,' she said, 'is that people will find this baby one day and say it was mine.' She spoke as though it was a sad inevitability, one more aspect of her life that would be misunderstood. Perhaps that is another reason why this story should be told.

With the soil levelled out, we looked around the garden for something to mark the grave. There was a loose paving stone near the edge of the lawn. I placed it on top of where we had laid Natalia to rest, and then we returned to Apartments 8 and 9.

The princess was quiet that evening in her sitting room: neither the television nor any music were turned on, which was unusual for someone who hated the silence of her home. She kept returning to the window that overlooked the garden, as if she was checking on Natalia, that the spot remained undisturbed.

I didn't go back into the garden for several days. When I did, it was clear that the princess had been there before me: a bunch of fresh flowers, that had been taken from my pantry, lay on the stone.

Throughout that summer, the princess continued to place flowers on the grave in memory of Natalia. Until her death in August 1997, she would remark on the garden's 'special stillness', and it is my belief that the grave has remained undisturbed to this day, as it should be.

For me, that ceremony remains a poignant memory of life at KP. I treasured it with the letter the boss wrote to me that evening, and left in my pantry on the blotter. She wrote:

Dear Paul,

Thank you so much for providing the support and sensitivity that was required today. It meant a great deal to the parents to have this very private moment and I did want you to know how grateful I am for the trouble you took.

Yours sincerely,
Diana

*   *   *

The princess only ever won one award, and it took pride of place in Kensington Palace. In 1995, a tall, thin shard of crafted glass, the United Cerebral Palsy Humanitarian of the Year Award was presented to her by Henry Kissinger at a glittering ceremony in New York in recognition of her humanitarian work. It made her feel so proud. She was praised publicly that night for identifying herself with and working tirelessly for 'the sick, the disadvantaged and the suffering'. It was her Oscar, if you like, and she made sure it was on display in the equerry's room on the ground floor of KP, a permanent reminder to herself. Finally, she had something to show for her contribution, something more worthy than the silver swimming trophy she had won in her schooldays. I think she felt she had actually achieved something of honourable distinction. It mattered to her because she was a true philanthropist, to whom compassion came naturally; it was an intrinsic part of her complex character.

From an early age, she had an empathy with those who were troubled or afflicted, and she often said that even in childhood she had felt the urge to reach out and help. At West Heath boarding-school in Sevenoaks, Kent, she didn't think twice about becoming a volunteer at nearby Darenth Park, a Victorian hospital for the mentally and physically handicapped. There, she was in her element, communicating with the patients, ignoring the intimidating atmosphere that made other volunteers withdraw. She had embraced her role with a confidence that belied her years, and she had learned then that just by holding someone's hand, she could help, cheer, calm or reassure. She would also visit an old people's home to make cups of tea. Even as a teenager, she was touching hearts and souls. As a princess, she said privately, 'I want to go where hearts need mending,' and broke a taboo when she held the hand of an AIDS sufferer in 1987, when an ignorant world believed the disease could be caught from the skin. She alerted the world, too, to the sufferings of landmine victims in Angola, because she wanted the maiming and killing of innocents to stop. She died with so much more to do. Even so, I think she brought about a change. The Ottawa Treaty, agreed in December 1997, was signed by several governments, creating an international ban on the use of anti-personnel landmines, and in commending the Landmines Bill 1998, to the Houses of Parliament, the late Robin Cook told MPs: 'All Honourable Members will be aware from their postbags of the immense contribution made by Diana, Princess of Wales, in bringing home to many . . . the human cost of landmines. The best way in which to record our appreciation of her work . . . is to pass the Bill, and to pave the way towards a global ban on landmines.'

Had the boss lived until she was a hundred, her work would never have been finished as she had an unquenchable desire to help the sick, the poor, the infirm, the abused, the addicted, the drunk, the homeless, the starving. 'I feel I can help them,' she would say. She believed passionately that she could make a difference. And she did, perhaps without realizing it.

That moment when she held the hand of a man infected with HIV changed public opinion, and lessened public fear. Former US President Bill Clinton summed it up best when, at the Diana,

Princess of Wales Lecture on AIDS in December 2001, he said, 'In 1987, when so many believed that AIDS could be contracted through casual contact, Princess Diana sat on the sickbed of a man with AIDS and held his hand. She showed the world that people with AIDS deserve not isolation but compassion and kindness. It helped change world opinion, and gave hope to people with AIDS.'

His speech chimed with words that the princess had written, about five years previously: 'I will always bring love wherever I go in the world, to whomever: leper, AIDS patient, king, queen or president.' She had been jotting down ideas for the future as we discussed potential humanitarian missions and charity projects. She was writing down her aims and hopes, expressing how she had 'an abundance of love and understanding for those in need'.

She treated everyone, of whatever status, in the same way. I thought she had more love to give lepers and AIDS patients than kings or queens. In my experience, she had less patience with kings and queens. She was instantly at one with the people who adored her, the ordinary men and women on the street. 'That's why the suits don't like me—because I get on better with the people 'downstairs' than I do 'upstairs'. We're all equal, regardless of where we've got to in life. Daddy taught me that,' said the princess.

Her ability to get on with anyone in any situation meant there was never any awkwardness with those she met on royal engagements and walkabouts. Whether she was consoling a close friend or a complete stranger, the princess's compassion was handed out with the same heartfelt tenderness.

64

She was no healer, and she brought no cures, but Susie Kassem said that the boss sprinkled invisible fairy dust wherever she went.

Among others, she would quote from the work of the Islamic poet Muhammad Iqbal, whose words she wrote out in her own hand, on the back of an official HRH Princess of Wales memorandum sheet. I saw it every time I walked into her sitting room because she stuck it to one of the square panes in the Georgian window that overlooked the walled garden: 'There are many who love God . . . they roam the jungles in their search . . . but I will love that person who loves all of God's humanity— Iqbal.' Whether she was in a hospital, an old people's home or a hospice, that belief guided her, it was never an obligation of duty for her, it was only ever a genuine pleasure of her role.

She always said that she got her 'people skills' from her father. Diana Spencer was born to be a great communicator and humanitarian. She was born to make an impact that could never be forgotten. And the effect she had on some people's lives was immeasurable.

*   *   *

The princess would often say that if you could make a difference to just one person's life each day 'then *what* a difference you could make!' And she set out to do just that.

She received hundreds of letters each week via the court post office at Buckingham Palace. Many envelopes were marked simply 'Princess Diana, London,' and a little red van pulled up at the back door of the apartments each day with a sackful of

65

fan mail. The daily letter mountains would be opened and sifted through by the princess's personal assistant, then sorted into different categories: official requests, charities and general public. Usually the assistant or a lady-in-waiting would reply on the princess's behalf, but now and again, when the boss's curiosity got the better of her, an odd letter would command personal attention.

One such letter was penned by a young girl, who had written about how her father couldn't get a job. He had attended dozens of interviews, he was a good man who deserved a job and 'her mummy and daddy had no money', she said. Could the princess use her powers to help find her dad a job?

It was an impossible request, and one to which others might have felt unable to respond, but the princess always knew what to do, and could always find a way of instilling hope in even the most desperate situations.

At that time, one of her favourite outfits was a navy-blue Escada trouser-suit, which she wore with a white shirt and a navy blue tie with an elephant motif. Within seconds of reading that letter, the princess had hurried into her dressing room and picked out that tie: in Hinduism, 'Ganesh', the elephant-headed God, is worshipped as the remover of obstacles and viewed as a helper in the attainment of success. The Indian community in London had presented to her a gold pendant of Ganesh, which she kept in her jewellery box. It was a symbol of good luck, she told me. She sent the tie to the little girl with a note: 'Thank you so much for your letter. Would you give this tie to your father to wear at his next interview to bring him luck?'

I never did find out whether Ganesh removed the obstacles for that family but I'm sure the tie gave that father a stronger resolve, and that the child ran about with giddy excitement when the royal reply dropped through her letterbox. I hope that that family has kept the princess's tie as a treasured memento.

Another letter from the general public's correspondence focused on the daughter of a fireman and his wife who lived in the south of England. The child had been born with a hole in her heart, and had become very poorly; the mother had asked for a signed photograph of the princess because her daughter was a big fan. A black-and-white image was sent out in a leather frame, bearing the monogram 'D' with a coronet. But the mother received much more than that: the princess was so moved by her letter that she picked up the telephone and rang her. I wish I could have been there when the lady picked up the phone to find the Princess of Wales at the other end of the line. Not that the boss ever referred to herself as 'princess', she would have asked to be called 'Diana'. Over the coming weeks, she telephoned the mother several times. Tragically, the little girl's condition deteriorated and she died, and I remember the princess on the phone, counselling the parents, talking them through their grief. There was little she could have done to improve the child's health—she was as powerless in that regard as the parents, the doctors and nurses—but she *did* make a difference. She brought a smile to the little girl's face when she opened the envelope to find a signed photograph, wishing her well, from

'Diana'. The boss shed a tear when the mother told her, at the funeral, that their daughter's treasured photograph had been placed beside her in the coffin. Nothing could have struck a more sensitive chord: the princess knew all about the significance of burying a loved one with treasured possessions. When her beloved father had died in 1992, she told me that her family had ensured he was dressed in his coffin in his favourite clothes, and she had placed with him some treasured, personal objects. It was, she said, a final act of love that was of vital importance to her. It is comforting to know that your loved one is surrounded in death by familiar, meaningful objects and I understood this. When my mother, Beryl, died, I did exactly the same: I placed a cigarette and a match with her so that she could have a last smoke, an unused bingo ticket so that she could have a last game, photographs of the grandchildren she would never see grow up, and letters from family and friends who wrote to say goodbye. It was about 'us' going on that journey with Mum. Others may find it odd, but it mattered to us as a family in the same way that it mattered to the princess and to the family of that little girl.

And because it had mattered, I knew what one of my most essential duties had to be when the princess died.

*   *   *

The princess told me she had found her mission in life in Calcutta in 1992 when she visited Mother Teresa's home for the sick, the starving and the dying, the same year in which her collaboration with Andrew Morton on his book *Diana: Her True*

Story emerged and led to an exchange of frank letters between her and the Duke of Edinburgh, and to her separation from Prince Charles. She suddenly discovered a stronger, independent self. With a sense of new-found freedom and identity, she embraced the chance to take on a new role.

She believed that: 'The self must know stillness before it can discover its true song', and 1992 was when she discovered that song during a life-changing experience in Calcutta, which steered her on to a more humanitarian and spiritual path. Calcutta had a profound effect on the boss, and she came away believing she had a mission to help the sick and the dying wherever she was in the world. It was her responsibility, she said, to make a difference.

She wrote down her thoughts and emotions about that trip to India in a vivid account, explaining the spiritual awakening she had experienced. When I accompanied her on her mission to Angola in 1997, to highlight the plight of the world's forgotten landmine victims, she presented me with a copy of her 'Calcutta story', as if she wanted me to understand her work and aims. I read and re-read the princess's words, written in her own hand, on the flight to Angola, and learned much about her. Here I have reproduced some in the hope that others, too, can understand the compassion she was eager to spread. It also provides a fascinating insight into her view of death, and the importance of 'dying with dignity'. It was written in 1992 on blue-embossed Kensington Palace writing-paper:

Today, something very profound touched my

life—I went to Mother Teresa's home in Calcutta, and found the direction I've been searching for all these years.

The sisters sang to me on arrival, a deeply spiritual experience, and I soared to such great heights in spirit. The light shone from within these ladies, saints for want of a better word— such love came from their eyes and their touch was full of warmth.

She wrote about Mother Teresa's home for children who had been abandoned or were malnourished.

TB was common amongst these little people. I picked up a little boy who was blind and deaf— I hugged him so tightly hoping he could feel my love and healing coming through.

Then she moved on to the hospice for the dying, where she felt the greatest impact as she stood among hundreds of beds crammed with sick men and women.

. . . some crying, some sleeping and some dying—dying with dignity with a 'carer' beside them. I knew the individual was so happy to be leaving this earth plane under Mother Teresa's roof—probably the first time in their lives that someone had cared for them, ironically at the end.

What an enlightening experience for me—it felt so right to be there beside these sick people as they prepared to finish their stay on this universe. The emotion running through that hospice was very strong and the effect it had on me was how much I wanted and longed to be a part of all this on a global scale. I have a deep feeling of a Mission to be fulfilled—it has set me apart from others for a long time now—I had my questions answered in Calcutta & I wish that it was possible to put my true feelings on to paper, but they run too deep and would frighten those around me by their intensity . . .

On my return to the UK, I am a changed person once again . . . I've learned a great deal & my energies are restored to even greater strength. I have an enormous amount inside me that I want to share with those who suffer or those who require light in their dark existence . . .

Unbeknown to her, she had only five years to do it, but she trod that path with vigour, determined to make a difference, even when her critics sniped and doubted, even when she was accused of political meddling over landmines, even when some quarters of the media said it was a publicity stunt.

Her Calcutta story, detailing her innermost thoughts and hopes, may appear mawkish and overly dramatic, but she was attempting to make sense on paper of what she had witnessed, and the impression it had made on her. Those were her genuine thoughts and feelings and how she viewed her role in life. Calcutta had a profound effect on her, and whenever she talked about it, tears welled in her eyes.

Unlike those who scoffed at her well-placed intentions, I witnessed at first hand the gentle touch of the princess who wanted to become known as 'The Queen of Hearts'. I saw what she was capable of, and how well she interacted with others, bringing calm, reassurance and hope with the simplest words and gestures. There was the mother who had lost her eighteen-year-old son in the former Yugoslavia's civil war, the princess took time out of a busy schedule in Sarajevo to join her at his graveside—as she was driving by she had seen the mother tending his grave, laying fresh flowers. There was also the blind and severely handicapped four-year-old girl, again in Sarajevo, whom the princess had found lying on a stinking, soiled mattress in her 'home'—a shell of bricks topped with corrugated-iron sheeting. The boss had picked her up and stroked her arms and legs, providing love and warmth that her parents could not because they weren't there. Landmines had killed them.

Sometimes the greatest moments took place nearer to home, and there was one young man— and many moments—whom the media never learned of. The princess visited the Royal Brompton Hospital in west London and touched the life of 'John the Greek' who, in turn, touched her heart. John, whose name was actually Ioannis, had been waiting for a lung transplant because he had cystic fibrosis; he was in London receiving treatment, sponsored by the Greek government. She had come across this frail young man on a previous hospital visit, and she said the moment she saw how much her visits meant, she wanted to be there for him. And so, at least twice a week for more than a year, I drove her to the hospital armed with a bag of goodies: CDs, videos, magazines, sweets, all seized from the reserves of William and

Harry.

'And who's the lucky man?' I'd ask.

'John the Greek,' the princess would say.

It was always late at night, past ten o'clock, when she made those visits. Always late, always dark, when the hospital was least busy, there was less chance then of her being spotted coming and going in the dark. She never used the main entrance. I always parked on a slip-road at the back so that she could nip in, undetected, through the emergency exit. Then I would sit and wait. She would be gone for at least an hour, sometimes accompanied by Susie Kassem. The princess would perch on the corner of the young man's bed, chatting about her boys, about her love of Greece, and about John's ambitions. He had been a law student before his illness. All that conversation helped him learn English because he wasn't fluent in the language. On one occasion, she took Prince Harry to meet the 'exceptional young man'. She spoke of his 'aura and humanity' and was much impressed by his courage. I don't think he ever had the strength to get out of his bed during her visits and yet, she told me, he never stopped smiling.

Often, on the journey back to the palace, she would sit in silence. It seemed so unfair to her that a young man of such potential faced such a bleak future unless a donor was found. Tragically, a donor was not forthcoming and John passed away. The princess was heartbroken: she had become very attached to him. It annoys me that people can doubt her motives, and dare suggest that her hospital visiting was some kind of ploy to enhance her image. She felt people's suffering and she cared genuinely. She felt the loss of 'John the

Greek' so deeply, but she wept in private. That is not the reaction of someone 'playing the angel card' as some in the media put it.

The princess took time out of her busy schedule to fly from London to Greece to be at his funeral. She wanted to be with his family—whom she had never met—because she was keeping a promise. On one of her many hospital visits, she had told John that if the worst happened, she would attend his funeral.

She was there for him right up to the end, as she had been in 1991 for her friend Adrian Ward-Jackson, whose death prompted the start of her campaigning to increase awareness about AIDS. 'Not since TB has there been a disease killing people *before* their parents, and no other member of this family [the Windsors] has taken it up,' she said at the time.

The princess had given Adrian her word that she would be with him at the end, and she sat with him for four days, with their mutual friend Angela Serota, as his life ebbed away. It was then that she learned how people face up to death and 'the journey of the soul'. Death didn't frighten the princess: from that intensely emotional moment, she developed a spiritual belief that the soul may linger invisibly on this plane, as she put it. That belief supported her on many occasions in her life, and it kept me standing when that terrible day came in 1997.

LEADING MEN, LEADING LADIES

The chauffeur-driven limousine swept us up into the Hollywood Hills, leaving behind the basin of the LA metropolis, then took us through huge electric gates towards the front door.

'How good to see you Mr Burrell,' said a smartly dressed gentleman as he opened the car door. 'You, too, Victoria,' he added, kissing the daughter of Yul Brynner, as she stepped from the vehicle. We entered a Californian ranch-style mansion, which was already alight with excitement. It was Oscars' night, and this was one of the pre-ceremony parties to attend.

Stretched out before me was a scene not dissimilar from a gathering before a British state banquet: a long, ground-floor room, with mirrored doors at one end, was filled with the famous and the beautiful, men in black tie, women in their finest gowns, Jimmy Choos seemingly on every female foot; and a brigade of liveried servants weaving through the guests, holding silver trays with champagne and canapés. Guests sat on oversized sofas in front of large stone fireplaces. There were directors, actors, actresses, agents, publicists, all guffawing, gossiping and small-talking; everyone observing everyone else. I pinched myself as a glass of champagne was thrust into my hand by a well-groomed butler. Then I was approached by our host's son. 'My mother isn't feeling well tonight, Paul, but she would like you to go upstairs and see her in her room.'

I found myself climbing a grand staircase, as wide

as the one at Buckingham Palace, and the social buzz faded as I walked along a corridor until I came to an open door. This was to be my audience with the Queen of Hollywood.

I walked into an all-white, sparsely decorated bedroom and, as I stood there, I was reminded of my early days as footman to Her Majesty the Queen, trying not to be overawed, trying not to stare, trying not to be agog.

Elizabeth Taylor, in a white gown, was reclining on her bed, propped up among a nest of plumped cushions. She was watching live coverage of the Oscars on an enormous, free-standing television screen. She turned her head and smiled a warm welcome. What struck me was the intensity of her eyes, and the shock white of her cropped hair.

Victoria Brynner, Miss Taylor's goddaughter, joined me, and Miss Taylor beckoned me closer with a wave of the hand. I approached her, and stood as close to the bed as possible, my knees just brushing the mattress.

Suddenly she turned to the television, and started to clap. 'Jack! Yes! Jack!' she shouted.

Jack Nicholson was walking on to the stage to receive his Oscar at the Shrine Auditorium for Best Actor in the movie *As Good As It Gets*. 'I voted for him—I *so* wanted him to win,' said the member of the Academy at my side.

She turned to face me, then patted the mattress. 'Are you in town for long?' I perched on the edge of the bed, feeling presumptuous and awkward, and explained I was in town for a week, and we started to chat with Victoria. If only the princess could see me now, I thought. She would be doubled up with laughter—a coal miner's son from

76

northern England, her butler, sat on Elizabeth Taylor's bed in the Hollywood Hills. I had spent my life in palaces, castles and royal residences and perhaps took it all for granted at times. In an actor's mansion, though, I was as awe-struck as I'd ever been.

The screen legend knew that I was in town—to be guest of honour at 'The Princess Ball' at the Beverly Wilshire Hotel, just off Rodeo Drive, to raise money for the Diana, Princess of Wales, Memorial Fund and the LA-based beneficiary charity, Aid for AIDS. It was March 1998, and Miss Taylor had agreed to be an honorary board member in support of the event. Hollywood names were backing it in honour and memory of the boss.

After my bedside audience, Miss Taylor allowed me to pick up and hold two of her three Oscars— for *Who's Afraid of Virginia Woolf?* and *Raintree County*.

It was a surreal evening that ended at the *Vanity Fair* post-Oscars party at Morton's restaurant where I was a guest of the magazine's editor-in-chief, Graydon Carter. That night was a whirlwind: I met Sharon Stone, Kim Basinger, Alec Baldwin, Matt Damon and Minnie Driver, and was proud to be introduced to them as 'the butler to Diana, Princess of Wales'. Everyone I spoke to, from the A-list to the sound experts, wanted to talk about the boss. It was as if her charisma was present in every room. It was six months on from the terrible events in Paris, and I remember feeling choked at the thought of how she'd have laughed with self-conscious embarrassment at the famous of Hollywood talking so fondly about her.

At the ball later that week, more names turned

out to remember her, including Jane Seymour, Gary Oldman, Jacqueline Bisset, Angela Lansbury, Rod Stewart and his then wife Rachel Hunter, and *Dynasty* star Linda Evans. The tabloids poked fun at the occasion, saying it was the night the stars *didn't* turn out, but it was a memorable evening for those who came to commemorate the princess. And in the week when Oscar-winner Jack Nicholson was the talk of the town, I recalled a story about the day he came face to face with the princess.

*   *   *

After she had been staying at the Carlyle, on her last visit to Manhattan, the princess returned to KP full of excitement. 'You'll never guess who I bumped into!' she said, eager to tell. 'Jack Nicholson!' If her reaction was anything to go by, the man was a master at working his charm, and clearly unfazed by British royalty. She told me how their meeting was brief, and they had exchanged pleasantries. But afterwards Mr Nicholson had sent her a handwritten note saying what a delight it had been to meet her and 'it would have been wonderful if we could have found time to have dinner'.

'A dinner date with Jack Nicholson!' she squealed. He was an interesting and charismatic man, she said, and she 'understands why so many women had fallen for him'.

Another Hollywood star who was determined to keep knocking at the door of KP was Tom Cruise. He had arrived in London for the Royal Film Premiere of his movie *Far and Away* at the Odeon,

Leicester Square, in 1993. The princess had long looked forward to the evening, and had taken hours to get ready, wanting to look her best. When she arrived in a halter-neck cream evening gown, she found herself seated in the front row beside Tom Cruise, with his co-star and then wife Nicole Kidman on the other side of him. And it seemed the actor had eyes for only one woman. 'He hardly spoke to me at all!' said an indignant princess, when she arrived home that night. 'He was all over her like a rash. They couldn't keep their hands off each other. It was the height of rudeness,' she said. The ego of the most beautiful woman in the world was, to say the least, a little bruised.

What she did not know was that Tom Cruise—who had also starred in *Top Gun* and *Rainman* by the early nineties—was determined to make it up to her. He would have been mortified to think he had been rude at the premiere because he is a gentleman who knows how to treat a lady. What surprised me was that his famous self-confidence had deserted him when it came to approaching the boss, and he was, we were told, too shy to ring the palace in person and ask the princess to dinner. Instead, he got a mutual friend to act as go-between and write a letter on his behalf. The princess showed me the letter, and she decided to write back, politely declining.

Tom Cruise, who in those days had a house complete with a chef in north London, persisted. He didn't take 'no' for an answer. What he lacked in confidence, he made up for in tenacity. A month later, a second written request arrived.

Now, before the media gets over-excited about this communication, it is worth stressing that it was a purely innocent, platonic invitation to drinks and dinner from someone who admired the princess. There was never any hint of romantic intention on his or the boss's part. Ultimately, the princess relented—she knew that Nicole Kidman wouldn't be there to steal all his attention! She had an enjoyable evening, and he spoke fondly about his wife to the princess. She remarked afterwards how 'very much in love he is' and I think she came away yearning to feel the same kind of happiness.

Another famous Tom—Tom Hanks—had a private line direct to KP. On a few occasions I put through a call from the Oscar-winning actor, ringing from New York or Los Angeles. He and Steven Spielberg were friends of the boss.

In 2004, when I took part in ITV1's *I'm A Celebrity . . . Get Me Out Of Here*—based on survival in the Australian jungle—I took a lot of stick for name-dropping about Tom Hanks, especially when the editing of the show made it appear that I'd talked about him non-stop!

But the fact is that this 'big name' of Hollywood—that was how the boss referred to famous people—was friendly to me in the months after her death. He must be one of the most approachable and down-to-earth figures in the entire movie industry. I'll never forget the time when, at four o'clock in the morning while I was asleep at home in Cheshire, the phone rang. He was on location in Fiji, where he was filming *Castaway*, and had been flicking through his address book, he said, and decided to give me a call to make sure I was doing okay. The man is a gentleman, and the princess thought so, too. In fact, after she had seen his 1994 movie *Forrest*

Gump, she reinvented the famous 'Run, Forrest, run!' line as 'Run, Paul, run!' whenever I had a hurried duty to perform at KP.

The world already knows the story of how she turned down a chance to star in *The Bodyguard II*, after a phone call from Kevin Costner. She even turned down a chance to be featured in a Warner Brothers limited-edition piece of animation artwork in 1994, an offer that came about because my friend Chuck Webb, who was working at the studio's gallery, had been approached with an idea from the vice-president of animation. They wanted to create a 'Princess Diana version' of an animation called 'We Are The Tunes' where a celebrity was photographed, surrounded by Warner Brothers' characters. A limited edition featuring Quincy Jones on a conductor's podium had been a huge commercial success in the fine-art market. If the princess took part, the studio would donate all proceeds to a charity of her choice. It was up to me to approach her with the idea, and she would be featured in a scene of her choice, I explained. 'Like a nursery with children!' I said. She described it as 'a funny and interesting idea' but she declined—she didn't think the Queen would be terribly amused if her daughter-in-law was to appear in a picture alongside cartoon characters.

*   *   *

Since my previous book, it has been suggested that the princess had an affair with John F. Kennedy Jr. The truth is that the princess met JFK Junior in New York in 1995, but it was a purely business relationship. He was 'sparkling company', she said, as he tried to persuade her to give an exclusive interview for his magazine *George*, but she declined, and put distance between them when he became increasingly persistent. The princess even doubted his 'intellectual fibre' so the idea that they had an affair, as was suggested in June 2005, is laughable. When the princess travelled to New York and stayed at the Carlyle, she usually visited someone else, a special someone who led her to fantasize about the idea that it might be possible for Diana, Princess of Wales, to become the First Lady of the United States of America.

'Can you imagine, Paul, me coming to England as First Lady on a state visit with the President and staying at Buckingham Palace?' She laughed when she articulated a thought that wasn't as far-fetched as some people may think.

All her friends had agreed that *anything* was possible since June 1994 when Prince Charles confessed on television, in a documentary made with the broadcaster Jonathan Dimbleby, that he had committed adultery with Camilla Parker Bowles, setting the royal couple hurtling towards inevitable divorce. From that moment on, slowly and reluctantly, the boss learned to let go of the past, and attempted to find elsewhere the happiness she deserved. Divorce ended fifteen years of marriage on 28 August 1996, but for some time before that, the princess had been wondering which direction to take in life, toying with moves to South Africa, Australia and America—and that was where my safe money would have been placed.

For a time in the States, she moved in the right circles of power and influence, mixing with and wowing the upper and political classes. She counted on the social company of Anna Wintour, of *Vogue* magazine, Katharine Graham, of the *Washington Post*, Tina Brown, of *The New Yorker*, and Barbara Walters, doyenne of US television. Her closest American friend was the businesswoman Lana Marks, who has her own handbag boutiques in London, Paris, Rome and on Rodeo Drive, in Los Angeles.

The husband of her greatest friend, Lucia Flecha de Lima, was the Brazilian ambassador to Washington by then, which ensured the boss remained politically well connected. She'd enjoyed private conversations with Henry and Nancy Kissinger, and Colin Powell. In many ways, whether in New York or Washington, the princess found life intoxicating there, and the people of America less judgmental.

She shared the White House fantasy with Lucia Flecha de Lima, as well as with me. The two ladies would imagine it together, and Lucia—who knew the lay-out of the White House—said she already knew which guest bedroom she would choose. The princess, either with Prince Charles or on her own, had long been a visitor to the White House, visiting the Reagans, the Bush Seniors and the Clintons. In the final year of her life, she organized a breakfast meeting there with Hillary Clinton. 'You never know, I might even get a glimpse of Bill!' she said mischievously, before she departed on that trip.

The then First Lady told England's princess that the American people would embrace her if she ever moved across the Atlantic, which fuelled the boss's desire to make the move to America, and, even, one day into the White House itself. She had it all dreamed out in her head—how she would decorate the presidential apartment, and become 'the new Jackie O'. But the dream wasn't supported by a liaison with a Kennedy. It was because she had built up an exceptionally close relationship with a politically well-connected billionaire—a significant figure in the American financial and business world. She had met the never-married, silver-haired bachelor during the Wimbledon tennis tournament in 1994, at a dinner hosted by Lord Rothschild. They had hit it off immediately, sharing a mission to help the poor and starving around the world. In fact, the tycoon would invest $100 million in a programme to help the poor. Based on their private conversations, the princess felt that he was capable of running for office. He knew both Bill Clinton and Donald Rumsfeld and the offices of his empire towered above the Manhattan skyline, overlooking Central Park—the view from that man's window was truly magnificent. I know because I've stood beside his desk. '*What* a view!' I said, over and over again.

'Yes, and it's one I could never tire of,' he replied. Nor could he ever tire of the princess.

'With me beside him, and him beside me, how could we fail?' the princess said, back at KP.

Now, that *was* a love affair, and the reason I was in the man's office was because the boss had sent me on a plane from London to hand-deliver a letter—she trusted neither the postal system nor the fax. The connection they shared was intense, albeit on–off. He could have provided her with everything, security, financial and personal support, a lifestyle with private jets (because he owned many), and even a possible future in politics.

I could tell that the liaison was becoming serious when this man's mother started to ring KP. The boss and she even met one afternoon in New York. It got to the point where the mother and I would have chatty conversations before I put her through to the sitting room. The boss also got to know his driver and secretary: his world and hers were beginning to interlock.

'What flowers should he send? Red roses?' his driver asked me one day.

'Oh, no,' I advised. 'Get him to send some long-stemmed yellow ones in a deep box.'

When they arrived, the princess was overjoyed. 'How romantic!' She beamed, while personally placing them into a vase. Romance was not something she had experienced much in her marriage.

Later that day, there was a call from New York. 'Have they arrived, Paul? Was she delighted?' His charm was working: the princess skipped faster and lighter on such days. But although she loved the man, he was a good deal older than she was, in his mid-fifties at the time. Ultimately, I think she became afraid of that age-gap, afraid of history repeating itself. That one doubt niggled away at her for months until she decided to draw a line under the relationship, and permanently shelved her hopes of a route to the White House. But when I was clearing out Apartments 8 and 9 after her death, I found a treasured photo of this person tucked into a secret place and remembered it all in an instant: the long-distance phone calls, the romantic candle-lit dinners at KP, the dates in New York. He was the one who got away.

One particular visit to the White House caused a sensation in the media on both sides of the Atlantic. 'DISCO QUEEN DIANA UPSTAGES JOHN TRAVOLTA' shrieked the *Daily Mirror* on 11 November 1985.

It was the night of a White House ball to herald the start of the Prince and Princess of Wales's first tour of the United States. At dinner, the princess was seated between President Ronald Reagan and the ballet dancer Mikhail Barishnikov. There could not have been a better selected dinner guest: the princess was a huge fan of Mikhail. As a teenager, she had stood outside the stage door of a London theatre to get his autograph, and he had signed it without looking at her. Yet there she was, returned to his company as the future Queen of England, and she was every bit as girly and giggly as she had been on the first occasion they had met. Ironically, it was Mikhail's turn to ask for a signature, passing a menu for her to sign. But the princess wanted more than an exchange of autographs—she wanted to dance with the great man on the chequered marble floor at the White House, to take centre-stage with her idol.

That was when it was arranged for her to dance with John Travolta and one of the greatest myths of that night was set in motion.

Wearing a Victor Edelstein off-the-shoulder, Edwardian-style ink-blue velvet dinner dress, the princess danced with the Hollywood actor, twirling around the floor to numbers from the musicals *Grease* and *Saturday Night Fever*. The photographs of that night were published in newspapers the world over. Then she danced with President Reagan and Clint Eastwood. But all the time, she wanted to dance with Barishnikov. She hadn't longed to dance with Mr *Saturday Night Fever* but with the man who was to her the King of Dance. Yet the occasion was billed, and has been remembered since, as the evening when the princess fulfilled a dream on John Travolta's arm.

Indeed, the actor himself has helped perpetuate this belief, and will write about it in his autobiography, he has said. Already, on ABC television's chat-show *Enough Rope—with Andrew Denton* he has given his version of that historic moment: it was 'her wish, her only wish, in coming to the United States . . . to dance with John Travolta'. He explained: 'I'm at the White House when Nancy Reagan, the President's wife, came up to me and told me this secret, which was that the princess would love to dance, and it's her only wish in the United States. I didn't know until that night . . . but it was her dream and, apparently, it was her fondest memory of that world tour.' Earlier, he had gone on record as saying: 'I was at the lowest point of my career and yet, in that room, I felt like a frog who had been turned into a prince. We had the time of our lives.'

I have no doubt that they did, and that Nancy Reagan did tell John Travolta it was the princess's dream. Maybe it was all Prince Charles's idea. But, as the princess told me years later, it was never *her* idea. She told me: 'John Travolta was a gentleman and absolutely charming but he wasn't *my* chosen partner. I really wanted to dance with Mikhail Barishnikov that night.' We had been discussing it because I was helping her sort through the photographs on the grand piano in the drawing room. She was pulling old ones out of their frames and inserting new ones. There, among the family photos, was the image of her and John Travolta dancing. It was one of the pictures she didn't want to change. It was, she said, a special memory. 'Because it reminds me of the night I got to dine with Mikhail Barishnikov,' she said.

*   *   *

I think it's fair to say that, out of the dozens of guests who came to lunch at KP, Oprah Winfrey was among the favourites, and the princess could have sat chatting with her all afternoon and into the evening.

The two ladies enjoyed a lively lunch, and there was much laughter that afternoon around the table. As Hillary Clinton had, Oprah raised the subject of the princess moving to the United States. At the time, the boss was seriously contemplating Australia but it seemed that life, and people, were always nudging her across the Pond.

'We love America, don't we, Paul?' the princess said, as I stood on the edge of the proceedings, on hand for service.

'I'd pack my bags and go and live there tomorrow,' I said, which was when Oprah made a quip about needing a good butler in Chicago.

Not everyone was seen as such good company— like the British journalist and broadcaster the boss considered 'sex on legs'. Until he came for lunch. 'He was a *big* disappointment!' she said afterwards.

In his defence, many visitors, especially men, were nervous in the company of the boss. She was disarmingly beautiful, and I'd seen politicians and Fleet Street editors reduced to quivering wrecks in her company. A bit like that particular guest.

'That was *the* most boring lunch I've ever had!' she went on.

She had watched him on television and thought he was witty, charming and intelligent. Perhaps he had an off day when he arrived at the palace, but I knew things weren't going well when the princess activated our discreet signalling system. She had a bell at her fingertips under the table—like one of those panic-buttons that bank-tellers have in case of armed robbery. No sooner had the starters been eaten than she had pressed the bell, which sounded as a muffled buzz in the lobby outside the dining room where I hovered. Serve. Eat. Sound the bell. Serve. Eat. Sound the bell. Each time I walked in, the princess flashed me the look that I knew meant 'hurry it up'. A three-course lunch plus coffee was served and cleared in just under an hour. And that was a first.

One star who fascinated the princess was Michael Jackson, as much for his upbringing and personality struggles as his talent. She endlessly played *Thriller* and *Bad*, thought he was 'absolutely amazing' and longed to meet him. The opportunity arose in 1988 when he came to Wembley on his *Bad* tour, and she invited Maria, with another dresser, to watch the concert with her and meet him backstage. She returned to KP with a selection of tour memorabilia for William and Harry: *Bad* baseball caps, jackets, T-shirts, pens. You name it, she'd been given it. The next morning, after I'd

89

heard from Maria what a brilliant time they had all had, the princess sat down to breakfast. If ever mystique was shattered by a personal meeting, this was it. 'It looked like his nose was about to drop off! The amount of surgery he's had!' she said, and she was surprised by how effeminate he was. But, she said, she loved him for his music not his looks, and it had been a 'thrill' to meet the man who made the music that filled KP until the day she died.

One favourite the princess failed to meet was the Hollywood screen legend Bette Davis. But it wasn't for want of trying. A combination of time and hectic diaries conspired to prevent an icon of royalty and an icon from an era of classical film ever coming together.

'Wouldn't it be fun to have Miss Davis round for tea?' said the princess when she learned that the actress who had twice portrayed Queen Elizabeth I, in *The Virgin Queen* and *The Private Lives of Elizabeth and Essex*, was in London to appear on Michael Parkinson's chat-show, promoting her book *This 'n That.* It was 1988 and I was butler to the Prince and Princess of Wales at Highgrove but I had been drafted to KP to cover Harold Brown's duties, while he was on leave. Those occasional times I spent as 'substitute butler' led the boss to draft me in more and more frequently, drawing me ever closer, until I moved permanently to west London in April 1993.

The princess had long been a fan of Bette Davis so she was excited to learn that she was in town and staying at the Dorchester. I had to make the call and arrange an appointment for tea. I thought it was only a matter of fixing a time, but the answer was a big let-down. One of the actress's assistants rang the palace to inform us that Miss Davis was only in town for a few days, hadn't been feeling particularly well (she had recently suffered a stroke), and her schedule was such that it was impossible to squeeze in a royal appointment for tea, but she would be 'delighted' to accept the invitation on her next visit to the capital. Sadly, Miss Davis never returned to London—she died in Paris the following year, 1989.

I shared the boss's disappointment because I, too, was a huge fan. It was why I had been so eager to help arrange tea, and that weekend she and I had chatted about some of Miss Davis's films: *Jezebel*, *Dark Victory* and *Now, Voyager*.

I shared with her a story of when Bette Davis had been disappointed by a missed opportunity herself.

During the Queen's tour of America in 1984, Miss Davis had been excited at the prospect of meeting the monarch at a dinner given in Her Majesty's honour at 20th Century Fox. At the time, I was footman to the Queen but on that occasion hadn't travelled with her. On her return, Sir Robert Fellowes, the Queen's private secretary, had told me about how he had sat next to Miss Davis at the dinner, which prompted me, as a fan, to write her a letter—on Buckingham Palace-headed stationery. The reply I received, dated 3 August 1984, summed up the actress's disappointment at having been unable to shake hands with the Queen.

We weren't even near enough to see how she looked. It was a heartbreak to one and all, especially since we went out of our way to wear white gloves. It made us feel that Her Majesty must have thought Hollywood actors and actresses were a bunch of 'social bums' . . . but I feel very thrilled when I look at your stationery and see the words 'Buckingham Palace'—

Bette Davis

She also sent me a personally autographed photograph, with the words 'For Paul Burrell, From Bette Davis', which hangs in pride of place at my home.

*   *   *

Part of the princess's fascination with the States was down to its people—be they A-listers or ordinary men and women. I would say that the postbag at KP was half filled with letters from America. Whether she was mixing in high-society circles in Washington or New York, or meeting people at ground level, she seemed to connect as easily with Americans as they did with her. I've never been able to put my finger on what it was, but perhaps a clue lies in an article, written for *Time*, by Nancy Gibbs and Priscilla Painton:

Diana played out an old American fantasy, the real-life fairytale. She was setting about the job of living happily ever after, a goal her sad-faced royal in-laws never seemed to entertain.

By the time she agreed to a divorce, she had embraced the American notion that marriage is more about self-fulfilment than sacrifice or lines of succession. She had built up such reserves of sympathy by this time that even as she lost her status, she kept her stature.

Sadly, that article was written after she had died but in the last year of her life she was embracing the idea of moving across the Atlantic to live the American dream; with the encouragement of Lucia Flecha de Lima, Hillary Clinton and Oprah Winfrey.

In the final days of August 1997, she knelt on the sitting-room floor and spread out a colour brochure and floor-plan of a cliff-top property in Malibu, California, overlooking the Pacific Ocean. It was the former home of Julie Andrews and Blake Edwards. That magnificent six-bedroomed property had already been laid on a plate for the princess: it was hers if she wanted it. As she invited me to kneel beside her to look at the plans, I had the distinct impression that this was a sneak preview of a 'done deal' for someone who had long been considering buying a holiday home abroad. It was why, in her final letter to me, she had written: 'Now, the tide is changing and we can all now have peace of mind and look forward to happier times and different homes. Thank you, Paul, for being such a tower of strength, love from Diana.'

With a finger that floated over the plans and took us room by room, she pointed it all out: 'And this is the main reception area. This is where William's room will be, and Harry's. And that annexe is where you will live with Maria and the boys.' She had it all worked out, and she expected her butler and his family to be part and parcel of that new life, moving into one of two guest cottages. I remember seeing white walls, an open-

93

plan interior and a red-tiled roof as the boss unfolded the brochure. It opened up into an enormous plan, like a giant tourist map.

News of the property emerged at my aborted trial in 2002, sourced from police statements in which I had detailed plans about a move abroad to establish my closeness to her, and prove that she was including me in her future, at a time when my position and her trust in me were doubted. Her future in America included me, as her final letter made irrefutably clear.

Until now, I have said little on those future plans. Indeed, in my previous book, *A Royal Duty*, I emphasized how the boss had suggested Cape Cod as a place to live 'if we don't live' in California. But even though she offered up the east coast as a second option, there was something certain in the way she spoke about a move to the west coast.

I have always said that I would stand in the corner of the princess and defend her memory and, where I could, ensure that history is recorded accurately. With that in mind, I feel I must now clarify what I know of the truth surrounding Julie Andrews's property because, over the following months—either around the inquest or the tenth anniversary of her death—I fear it will be suggested that the boss was intending to move into that property with Dodi Al Fayed, and the claim will be presented as fact by those whose interests are best served by the suggestion that Dodi was 'The One'. The details of that property were in a brown A4 envelope, which, after the boss had shown them to me, she placed on the window seat in her sitting room. The envelope was marked 'Harrods Estates'. I never saw it again but it was clear that the property had emanated from Harrods and, therefore, Mr Mohammed Al Fayed. I have learned since, from various reports, that the property had been bought by the Al Fayeds in June 1997—a month before the princess had even started 'dating' Dodi. And it is this that I fear might be hi-jacked as 'proof' that 'Dodi and Diana were planning to set up home together', just as it had been suggested that they were getting engaged, when they emphatically were not, that she told everyone she was pregnant when she was not, that the princess fell in love with Villa Windsor and was planning to move with Dodi to that Al Fayed-owned property in Paris when she loathed it—she described it as 'like a mausoleum'.

Because of all those myths, it is worth stating now that the princess made clear to me that the California house would only ever be a holiday home, to be used for up to six months a year. It was *not* to be a permanent home. She was keeping KP as her London base. William and Harry were *not*, to the best of my knowledge, made aware of the property and she *never* visited the Malibu mansion. At the time, I had been under the impression that the boss had been considering its purchase but it seems now that she was being offered its use, perhaps as part of a rental arrangement, by the Al Fayeds. More crucially, she made it clear that the property was for her, her family and guests. Had there been any hint of Dodi Al Fayed spending time with her in that multimillion-dollar residence she would have told her friends. And she did not.

As much as we could 'look forward to different homes', a specific property had not been finalized even though she was giving serious thought to the Malibu mansion. A decision would have been made when she returned from Paris. To me, though, she was still making up her mind about precisely where in America she wanted to spend time.

But why, as people will inevitably ask, was she thinking of moving into a property owned by Dodi.

It is at this point that I ask everyone to consider the basis of the 'Diana and Dodi love affair'. It was influenced and brought about by Mohammed Al Fayed acting as Cupid, with the same determination he has demonstrated in attempting to force history to accept them as 'a couple' because tragically, they died together. He was bent on ensuring that his son would obtain the love of the princess, and that was what I told Scotland Yard during its investigation into her death. I'm not doubting that the boss was swept away by the intoxicating jet-set lifestyle and the almost royal toys Dodi promised. He had already offered to buy her a silver Lamborghini. And when the princess accepted, after much persuasion, an invitation to join the Al Fayeds on holiday at a private villa overlooking a bay on the Côte d'Azur during that summer of 1997, Mohammed Al Fayed wasn't going to spare an inch of luxury: the next day he got out his chequebook and purchased a 200-foot yacht, *The Jonikal*, for an estimated £15 million.

Anything for Diana, Princess of Wales. Money was no object.

So, if he could spend £15 million on a yacht to wine-and-dine the boss for two weeks, the private offer to her of a $7 million mansion in Malibu to use as she wished would have been another act of generosity by a family renowned for its extravagant and lavish gifts. To me, a wealthy individual had understood the princess's need to find a property that offered privacy and high-level security. That house fitted with her plans, even if, perhaps, she didn't see the strings attached.

Whatever the circumstances, and whatever is claimed subsequently, let's douse the embers before the flames take hold. If the princess was near to accepting a kind offer to use the Malibu mansion, Dodi was *not* part of that picture.

Mr Al Fayed is still grieving for his son, and his sense of injustice is understandable, but the princess and Dodi had no more than a summer fling. In the final six telephone calls she made to her friends, and in the conversations she had with other people in the weeks before her death, she made it categorically clear that it was *not* a serious love affair, that she was desperate to cut short her time with Dodi and return home to see William and Harry, and that she was *not* even thinking about marriage. 'I want another marriage like I want a bad rash,' were her precise words, said to me and others.

There is not a shadow of doubt in my mind that, had the princess returned home, Dodi's days as her 'boyfriend' were numbered. Anyone who was close to the boss feels the same way. It is the consensus of those people who knew her inside out and, despite the boss's fondness for him, Mohammed Al Fayed didn't know her that well. The idea that she implicitly trusted him, and therefore confided in him, is ludicrous.

So for him to declare, 'She was pregnant . . . they told me,' doesn't make sense or ring true. When he speaks like that, he does nothing but a disservice to her memory and his son's.

With that in mind, there is another truth that must be told for the first time, to prevent another myth becoming accepted as fact and contributing to an inaccurate historical record. I have long grappled with, and struggled to balance, the private need to protect the princess's secrets with the public obligation to do justice to her memory. The line between the two is as thin as it is precarious to tread. I know that I'm damned if I do and damned if I don't whichever choice I make. If I divulge something I consider to be of service to her memory—and a true history—then I will stand accused of betrayal. If I do nothing and allow the myths to go unchallenged, I feel I'm betraying her interests. The choice becomes impossible to make when it revolves around one specific discussion in which she told me not to say a word to anyone else. In fact, her exact words were: 'I'm only telling you, Paul.'

In my mind, that was a command which is why I have said nothing until now. Indeed, it is why I have not been entirely open about an episode that took place less than forty-eight hours before her death.

Previously, in recalling my final conversations with the boss, I have detailed how she fretted about Dodi producing a ring when he had already showered her with a silver photo frame inscribed with words of love, a multi-stranded seed-pearl bracelet held at each end with jewel-encrusted dragons' heads, a diamond necklace, bracelet and earrings from Bvlgari, and a rectangular Jaeger LeCoultre Reverso wrist-watch.

Dodi had fallen in love. He told her so over dinner. Her reply, as I've said before, was polite but noncommittal and she thanked him for the compliment, a subtle non-reciprocation which she handled perfectly. But she worried about what might come next. Maybe it was instinct. Maybe she had learned of something but she asked: 'What do I do, Paul, if it's a ring?' It was a panicky question she had also put to Rosa Monckton.

That was when I offered her the advice: 'You accept it graciously and slip it on to the fourth finger of your right hand.' That way, it could only be seen as a friendship ring.

Fourth finger, right hand. We kept saying it, and she agreed that was what she would do. We talked about it in our penultimate telephone conversation. It is at this point that truth must now outweigh the need to protect one of her many secrets.

In my last book, I said we never had another conversation about that ring, and I didn't confirm whether or not it was actually produced. But that was a white lie aimed at stopping speculation that the princess had become engaged. If she had become engaged, she would have told me and her friends. So, by omission, I hoped the absence of a ring would quash the engagement rumours. But, increasingly, Mohammed Al Fayed has been fuelling those stories. More disturbingly, newspapers have given him column inches to air his views.

On 28 February 2006, the *Daily Mirror* allowed him to announce that Dodi had bought an engagement ring, and the couple were due to make an announcement in the first week of September.

'I know because they told me so,' he said.

It is clear that this ludicrous claim has also evolved into a serious line of enquiry with the officers at Scotland Yard investigating the death of the princess and Dodi Al Fayed.

'What right do people have to rubbish me?' Mr Al Fayed asked, in the *Daily Mirror* article.

The truth, which I have also detailed to Scotland Yard, is that Dodi *did* produce a ring, as the boss had feared. She told me so in our final conversation on 29 August 1997. She was on the deck of the yacht *Jonikal* and I was at the home of my brother-in-law in Cheshire.

She had done exactly as we had discussed and placed it on the fourth finger of her right hand. She made it clear that Dodi had given her a ring, but *not* an engagement ring, and she wore it as the gift was intended. It was nothing more than an addition to her collection of costume jewellery. Dodi had bought her nothing more than a dress ring.

I remember her saying it was a gold band, about how 'beautiful and lovely' it was, how 'kind and generous' he had been. The ring was from Bvlgari, she said, and was part of a suite of jewellery to match the necklace, bracelet and earrings he had already bought. She said how romantic he had been, and she giggled with relief that the ring hadn't been more significant. 'Pheeeew!' She gave an exaggerated sigh, suggesting that she was happy and that engagement was the furthest thing from her mind.

The boss had always laughed off talk of marriage into the Al Fayed family. It had been a long-standing joke between her and the Harrods owner, if not with Dodi. I remember one conversation we had after she'd visited Mohammed Al Fayed in his office on the fifth floor of his shop. 'God lives on the fifth floor!' she joked, as I drove her back to KP from Knightsbridge.

During that short journey, she also giggled about a flirtatious remark he had made as they said farewell. 'You're going to marry my son but it's Egyptian custom for the father to get in there first!' That was typical of his sense of humour, and the princess found it endearing, not offensive.

She had visited him to finalize arrangements for the summer holiday she would share with William and Harry at the Al Fayeds' villa on the Côte d'Azur, with the yacht *Jonikal* anchored nearby. During the holiday Mr Al Fayed asked his son, Dodi, to come and meet the princess on 15 July.

Six weeks later, he expects us to believe that the couple were ready for marriage.

It has long been a matter of dispute about whether the princess was getting engaged, and myth has told the world that Dodi had ordered and taken delivery of an engagement ring, which was never produced but was found later in his apartment.

Italian jeweller Alberto Repossi had, it appeared, provided support for Mohammed Al Fayed's assertion that the princess and Dodi had visited one of his boutiques and ordered a dazzling £130,000 engagement ring from a collection called 'Tell Me Yes'.

In June 2006 it was reported that, in an American television interview, Mr Repossi had said that no *engagement* ring had ever been bought. But the engagement rumour still persists, and it angers me that Mohammed Al Fayed continues to want the world to accept this fantasy. But history cannot accept that black is white.

The inescapable truth is that she *was* wearing a brand new band when she died—and it would only have been worn on the fourth finger of her right hand.

It is emphatically the case that they weren't getting engaged, and Dodi produced a ring that made no commitment and promised no future. His own actions speak louder than any of his father's words, and it is those actions that history should remember.

It is wrong that Mr Al Fayed has tried to elevate this relationship into more than it was. If Dodi was a son who told his father everything, then I assume that he would have told his father that the ring he had bought was a relatively cheap, £3,000 Bvlgari band—not the £130,000 gaudy, Repossi engagement rock that Mr Al Fayed has publicly paraded.

The cold truth about Dodi is that, to the princess, he was an intense, short-lived fling. He only ever spent ten minutes at KP, and the boss had spent just 26 days in his company. She never rushed into making up her mind about any man, let alone someone with whom her connection was so shallow and fleeting. More importantly, when she died she was still in love with another man, the heart surgeon Dr Hasnat Khan—whose bond with her was far, far deeper and more spiritual than anything she shared with the Harrods heir.

Andrew Morton, the royal biographer who wrote *Diana: Her True Story In Her Own Words*, ends the revised edition of that book with these words: 'As

102

the years pass, fact will become myth, and myth will become reality, smothering the real Diana. In the battle for Diana's memory, as in all wars, truth is the first casualty.'

I can't allow truth to become a casualty, and for as long as the private, behind-the-scenes truth about what she and Dr Khan shared remains untold, then the Dodi myth will stand. And that cannot be allowed to happen if I am to serve her best interests.

That is why I think it is time for the true love story to be told; and why I now find myself writing about a private relationship.

In that summer of 1997, the boss's heart still belonged to Dr Khan, the man she called 'The One'. Their relationship had broken up painfully, and she had met Dodi on the rebound.

Far from damaging or betraying her memory, the account I shall give celebrates a deep love, and shows the princess at her happiest. I shall not share all of the details because many aspects of their story should remain between the boss and Hasnat. But it is a love story that deserves to be told.

As for Dodi's ring, I would see it in the Paris hospital just two days after my final conversation with the boss.

'THE ONE'

'I can't find him. I *can't* find him!' There was a note of pleading in her voice. The princess was sobbing uncontrollably in the sitting room, clutching a handful of soggy tissues.

103

'I don't know *where* he is,' she said, as she perched on the edge of the sofa, rocking backwards and forwards in her white towelling robe, as vulnerable and as upset as I had ever seen. My heart went out to her.

It was the night of 15 September 1996, eighteen days after the divorce had become absolute. It was between eleven o'clock and midnight and I had been called up to KP from my home, at the Old Barracks in the palace grounds, by a frantic, tearful call. I had been about to go to bed, ready for another seven o'clock start the next day, when the phone had rung. Much to Maria's displeasure, I hurriedly got dressed and ran up to Apartments 8 and 9. As I've said, being there for the boss meant being on call twenty-four hours a day. It came as much with the friendship as it did with the job.

She was alone in a room softly lit by the cream silk-shaded lamps. The telephone, with its long, snaking cord which allowed her to walk with it from room to room, was at her side. Her mobile (the size of a brick in those days) rested beside her on a cushion. She was sipping a glass of water. I sat next to her and put my left arm round her shoulders. This was no time to stand on ceremony. This wasn't Diana, Princess of Wales, to whom I was offering comfort but the young Spencer girl. She leaned in to me, then sat up to explain. She didn't need to say much: we both knew what—and who—this was all about because of a conversation we'd had earlier that same day. It revolved around Dr Hasnat Khan, the man she was truly in love with, the man whom the inner circle of her friends referred to as 'The One'. It was a year since they had met in 1995.

'I've tried to contact him for five days now, and left messages everywhere. What more can I do?' she said, sniffling her way to composure. 'I've been to his flat—it's in darkness—I've left messages on his bleeper and at the switchboard, and I don't know where he is.'

Hasnat was an eminent heart surgeon who worked at the Royal Brompton Hospital in Chelsea. Whenever she left a message, she used the code-name 'Dr Allegra'—agreed between them. She also had a secret nickname for him: 'DDG', which stood for 'Drop Dead Gorgeous'. Sometimes we referred to him as 'Sleeping Beauty' because his late shifts meant he worked strange hours and sometimes slept till three o'clock in the afternoon.

But on that particular night he wasn't even answering to his first name. I tried to offer reassurance, as friends do, suggesting possible reasons for his silence to make her feel better, although I knew there had been a minor altercation in a telephone conversation the previous week.

'Perhaps he's so consumed with work that he's lost track of time,' I said, 'You know *him*, Your Royal Highness. He'll turn up when you're least expecting him!'

But none of what I was offering seemed to ease her upset. Then came the real reason for her calling me at such an hour. 'Can I ask you to go out and find him and deliver him a message?' she asked. She knew I'd say yes. 'You know where to look. Would you? Would you?'

There was no rejecting that hope. She could

105

hardly have gone out trawling the streets herself so, with my anonymity, it fell to me.

Within minutes, I was heading for the door. 'You will ring me as soon as you get back? I'll be up and waiting. It doesn't matter what time it is,' she said, then sent me out into the night.

West London was at its most quiet and I hailed a black cab to head for this man's flat in Kensington. I knew where he lived because I had visited him, with a message, on two previous occasions.

When I got there, he wasn't in. Next stop was his local pub. I had met him there for drinks on previous occasions. But there was only a landlord and a locked front door. I even went to the fast-food burger outlet I knew he used for supper-on-the-run but he wasn't there either. Then I remembered a wine bar where he knew the owners, I found it and went down the steps and through the door. There, in the corner at a square table filled with empty beer bottles and smoke that clung to your clothes, was the man I had been searching for, oblivious to the upset he had caused. He smiled when he saw me, as if my visit was reassurance for him, too, that he was being missed.

'You've no idea what trouble you've caused me,' I said, sitting down opposite him.

'Join me for a beer, Paul,' Hasnat said, and I did. We talked, and it transpired that this was a case of crossed-wires, a misunderstanding and paranoia that had bred in both of their minds. Over that beer, I delivered the message I had been given and he gave me a message from the heart to take back with me.

It was after one o'clock in the morning when another cab dropped me off at KP. Unknown to

106

me at the time, the princess had been bombarding Maria with calls at home.

'Is he back yet?'

'Why is he taking so long?'

'Please get him to call me as soon as he comes in!'

She had rung every half-hour, it emerged.

I didn't want to call her when I got back. I wanted to see her in person because the message was something that had to be said to her face. As I walked up the cobbled passageway and into the back of Apartments 8 and 9, I dreaded to think what the police would make of my comings and goings on the CCTV monitors.

The boss must have heard my footsteps on the staircase. 'Paul, is that you?' She was darting down the corridor, then waiting for me at the top of the stairs. 'Did you find him?' she asked.

'Yes, I did,' I replied, rather smugly, satisfied that Mission Impossible had been accomplished.

She scurried me into the sitting room and sat down on the sofa, all eager with anticipation. I sat on the chair opposite. I told her everything was fine, then delivered the message.

The face that had been so wretched a couple of hours earlier lit up with joy. She was high, secure and in love again. She thanked me, and thanked me, and thanked me. 'Now, you get home. Maria will be worried about you,' she said.

Maria will be bloody furious with me, I thought.

'I'll see you in the morning,' she said, as I started to switch off the lights. 'Night, Paul.' Those were often her final words to me every night.

'Goodnight, Your Royal Highness,' I said.

I got home and found Maria fast asleep, with the

phone beside her. She was curled up in a ball on the sofa.

The next morning, reporting for work at bang on seven o'clock, I reached my desk in the pantry and found a note from the boss, dated 16 September 1996, on her cream, burgundy-edged Kensington Palace writing-paper, complete with the monogram 'D' and a coronet.

It read:

Dear Paul,

Not many people would venture out late at night to sort a heart out on basically a strangers [sic] door! But then, not many people have the kindness and qualities you possess. I am profoundly touched by your actions last night, and very much wanted you to know that. Times are challenging in this particular home, but one thing is for sure, that is without you at the helm of this ship, we'd all be in bad shape and the laughter gone! So thank you very much for coming to my rescue once again, love from,

Diana

If my actions led to a new wave of happiness, then my duty, as friend and butler, was done. And 'happiness' is the crucial word: because with the man known as 'The One', she was almost levitating with happiness. With him, she was the happiest I had ever seen—and ever would see—her.

*　　　*　　　*

I had read the tabloid articles about 'Diana and Dodi' with dismay in those dizzy days of August 1997 as the boss cruised the French Riviera and Sardinia with Dodi Al Fayed on board the *Jonikal*. I remember the photo of her wearing white shorts over a black 'body' and carrying her white deck shoes, with Dodi walking behind her, and thinking, *She's not happy, there's no way she's happy*. That was the sentiment I expressed to Maria. I also remember a conversation with the boss when she rang me from the deck of the yacht.

'I'm ready to come home now,' she said, with a deep sigh. She'd enjoyed her 'bliss and fun' in the sun but was fed up with the summer fling and the gifts being pushed on to her. 'You've had enough of all the pampered luxury, then?' I asked, half joking. She sighed again. 'I just need to come home,' she said.

I don't subscribe to the convenient fairy tale that the boss died when she was at her happiest because it's not what I believe. 'Happy' and 'happiest' are two different feelings. Had the outside world been privy to the happiness she exuded when in the company of Hasnat, it would have been able to put into context the momentary joy she experienced with Dodi. But one smile from the boss, one embrace on the deck, was amplified into something more significant than it actually was by the camera lenses, focusing on snatched moments as the 'Diana and Dodi' relationship was played out like a soap opera. In comparison, her relationship with Hasnat had been exceptionally private and secret, nurtured behind the scenes, too precious and fragile to be exposed to the lenses. It was much too important to be thrown into the media circus, and I had never known her take such care over an intimate association with a man. I watched events unfold on the *Jonikal* with a knowing eye: I was aware of how adept the princess was at using the press to send signals. Referring to her humanitarian role, she once famously said, 'Being in the public eye all the time imparts a particular responsibility. Photographs, for instance, send a message to the world about an important cause and emphasize that message.' But she also knew the power of a photograph in sending out personal messages. She was an expert manipulator of the media, teasing them with her image. And some of those photos with Dodi that week were, I remain convinced, signals sent out to grab Hasnat's attention. He was the man she described privately as her 'soulmate'.

He was the *only* man she ever referred to as such.

Dodi was fun but Hasnat was her soulmate.

Every morning, I spread out the entire collection of national newspapers on the breakfast table in the dining room at KP. I can't remember a day when she wasn't featured in at least one—and she was fascinated by what the press and columnists were saying, and the 'angles' used for a royal story. But from 1995 onwards, she became interested in what one person thought of the coverage and the stunning images of her splashed across the front pages.

'I wonder what he'll say?' she'd ask. Or 'What will he think?'

She was determined to make an impression on Hasnat, a kind, sensitive, warm, modest man, and brilliant in his field. But he once told a little white lie—and this is how the 'messages' and 'signals' in newspapers began. He portrayed nonchalance over the media coverage of her, and said he never took much interest in what the papers said about her. But the princess knew otherwise: under his bed at his flat, she had found a secret stash of newspaper and magazine cuttings. All about her.

'You'll never guess what . . .' she said to me at KP, when she returned, and then she told me.

She thought it amusing that he had collected those clippings, as if he was proud of her. That he didn't want her to know was, perhaps, down to his endearing modesty. She kept that knowledge in mind whenever she was headline news. She *knew* he was taking an interest, regardless of what he said. She knew that, as she sat at KP with the newspapers in front of her, he was popping into his local corner shop on the way to work to buy a copy, just to check. She wanted him to be impressed, to be wowed, to be proud of the work she was doing, the speeches she made. She wanted him to sit up and take notice. And those pictures taken on the *Jonikal*—on the diving-board, in the sea, on the beach—were clear signals sent out to Hasnat; a 'flare' from the boat to arouse his jealousy. She was hardly in distress but her heart, I know, was still in London.

They say that a photograph never lies but those images of the princess and Dodi spoke the biggest untruths. Sadly, she never returned home to discover what response they had provoked in the person for whose eyes they were intended.

*   *   *

111

It was September 1995 when the princess first laid eyes on him, in one of those classic moments when lift doors are about to close and someone puts a foot between them, she told me. She was in the lift with a female friend at the Royal Brompton Hospital, and when it stopped at the first floor, the foot belonged to Hasnat. He was wearing his white coat, leading a group of student doctors. The moment she saw him there were sparks, she told me later. 'My heart nearly stopped!' she laughed.

It wasn't long before she fell deeply, and unexpectedly, in love. She ensured she had obtained his telephone number, and her visits to that building became constant. 'I have met the *most* wonderful man,' she would tell me and others, unable to contain her excitement. She adored his hands, his large brown eyes, his long eyelashes. 'Can you imagine what beautiful children we would make!' she winked. No other man stood a chance from the moment that highly educated and compassionate individual arrived on the scene. She was smitten from day one.

Oddly, I don't think he realized in those early days. He always felt he wasn't good enough, that he had nothing to offer but himself and, therefore, fell short. What he failed to understand was *that* was all she ever wanted—a man offering nothing but himself. He was the one man who didn't expect anything from her; there were no conditions attached and no underlying motive for the association. Indeed, he preferred to be 'secret'. He didn't want her money or fame, nor the adulation of standing by her side. He didn't overwhelm her with anything other than love. He wasn't infatuated or obsessed. He didn't have a father who had encouraged him centre-stage to play the role of boyfriend, like Dodi. It was why his love for the boss, and hers for him, was pure.

I've often wondered whether Hasnat's insecurities were down to the fact that, on the face of it, he and the boss were the most unlikely of couples, and that he doubted why such beauty was spellbound by him. He wasn't the fittest, slimmest or healthiest of men, and he was a heavy smoker who liked a good drink. The boss was immaculate, loathed smoking, ate healthily and was obsessed with keeping trim. He felt she could have had anyone in the world, so why him? But in all their time together, she never looked at another man.

I knew it was serious when the woman who detested smoking started buying ashtrays from Thomas Goode, Hermès and Harrods. They appeared in the sitting room, drawing room and dining room. Each morning, before I reported for duty, the princess had already emptied and polished them herself, removing all evidence of the previous evening's visit before the arrival of the rest of the staff or any friends. I'd find the ash tipped into the dustbin in my pantry, scattered on top of Kentucky Fried Chicken boxes. *This* must *be love*, I thought.

*   *   *

The BMW eased to a standstill in a dark corner of a cobbled lane in a quiet mews—an agreed meeting place. I sat behind the wheel, flicked off the headlights, and watched in the rear-view mirror for the shadowy approach of my passenger. Then I saw him, walking casually, swinging a plastic bag that contained dinner for two—a take-out from Kentucky Fried Chicken. The rear passenger door opened and Hasnat hopped in. 'Hello, Paul, how are you?'

'It's good to see you again,' I replied, and I headed back to KP having collected the boss's precious cargo.

He knew the routine. As we approached the palace entrance, he'd grab the tartan rug on the back seat, lie flat and pull it over himself, so that he was hidden from the two uniformed policemen on guard at the fourteen-foot-high iron gates. As I drove up to them, I'd flash the headlights three times—the signal to the police that it was me. I had told them on my departure that I'd be about half an hour, and they also recognized the registration plate. The barrier lifted and they waved me through, which allowed me to accelerate, thus giving them little chance to notice the bundle on the back seat. Instead of continuing to the top of the drive and bearing right to go to the front door of Apartments 8 and 9, I turned sharp right into King's Court—the route to Princess Margaret's front door. This was the ideal spot to usher inside secret guests because the Queen's sister had insisted that no CCTV cameras were to monitor *her* front door. The boss wasn't the only princess intent on ensuring that the comings and goings of her guests went undetected. That inner courtyard was the only blind spot within Fortress KP, and the two princesses used it to their advantage. Across the courtyard and opposite Princess Margaret's front door a secret passage led to the back entrance of Apartment 8, and that was where I would deposit my cargo.

The sound of a car engine always brought a twitch from Princess Margaret's curtains. 'She just *doesn't* miss a trick!' the boss would laugh.

The Queen's sister was always watching and observing from Apartment 1A, dead opposite. When I revisited KP in July 2006, the public tour took me to that very spot in Princess Margaret's home—the chequered black-and-white marble hallway. I couldn't help but lift the blind, just as she once had, to take a peek at the secret back door I had used so much. *So* this *was the view you had, Ma'am*! I thought, putting myself into her shoes. I visualized it there and then, as it had been almost ten years earlier. When I had pulled up in the car, our back door had been left ajar and the princess was standing there, beaming through the narrow gap. She couldn't wait to see Hasnat.

My passenger had thrown off the rug and jumped out; the princess opened the door a little wider to let him in. 'Night, Paul,' she said, chuckling, and waved as I walked back to the car.

Then she would make an exaggerated wave to the windows opposite, to the nosy royal she suspected was observing it all. 'Night, Margo!' she would shout. The boss knew that the Queen's sister was not talking to her at that time because she disapproved of her BBC *Panorama* interview, and that wave was intended to wind her up.

The back door closed, the twitching curtains fell back into place, and I turned the car out of King's Court, parked it at the front door, then went home for the night.

*   *   *

'I want him to spend more time here—to come and go as he pleases,' said the boss, as the secret relationship intensified in the summer of 1996.

Times were changing: her official separation from Prince Charles was moving towards divorce, and the princess had found what she had been looking for: her Mr Right.

'We could do something with the equerry's room,' she suggested one day.

That room, on the ground floor at the foot of the main staircase, had been somewhat redundant since the departure of Patrick Jephson, the private secretary. The room hadn't been redecorated since the Waleses had taken possession of the apartments in 1981. In the final year of her life, the boss was making plans for its refurbishment. 'We could make it lighter, find new sofas, put in a wide-screen television so he can watch football—even install a bar and a fridge. William and Harry could join him at weekends!' she imagined.

She wanted to turn the equerry's room into a 'den' for Hasnat. The highly significant fact that she saw the man in her life integrating with her sons tells the world all it needs to know about how much in love she was. He was the future for a woman who couldn't wait to escape her past.

He was introduced to William and Harry on several occasions. He wasn't a secret she felt she could keep from her boys, and she wanted them, more than anyone, to accept him. I'd like to think now that, with the knowledge taken from those meetings, those young men still remember how much Hasnat loved their mother, and how much he meant to her. I'm convinced that they know *he* was the real love in their mother's life, not Dodi.

The boss respected her boys' feelings in regard to Hasnat and allowed him into their world very slowly, as any mother would when she was stepping gingerly towards the introduction of a new man into the family. It was an uneasy and awkward time for William and Harry because they were coming to terms with their parents' divorce, and I think Harry found it particularly hard. But I remember William sitting down with Hasnat, having a mature discussion about his job and what he himself wanted to do with his future until Harry ran in, interrupting them with excitable talk about tanks, soldiers and aeroplanes.

The princess wasn't exactly planning for Hasnat to move into KP but she wanted to accommodate his needs whenever he stayed over. He was a regular guest, and it was surreal, early on, getting used to him wandering around the corridors and private rooms, making himself at home, late at night or first thing in the morning, and sometimes until three o'clock in the afternoon.

One of my essential duties was to ensure that the relationship was hidden from other members of staff and visitors. It was one thing smuggling him into the palace via the back door but it was another to keep him 'hidden' inside. It changed routines like never before.

Doors were closed, marked out of bounds. Suddenly there were 'electrical failures'—which enforced the transfer of the hairdresser from the dressing room to the sitting room. Masseurs found themselves setting up tables in there instead of in her bedroom.

Overnight, the princess became 'terribly hungry', and I had to ask the chef to send out double portions which I would divide and serve as dinner for two, in the dining room or on trays elsewhere. And the kitchen couldn't have failed to notice that she had developed a sudden passion for bacon sandwiches with HP sauce. For those with eagle eyes, the usual reserves of Montrachet white wine and Veuve Clicquot champagne were replaced with Budweiser in the wine refrigerator.

At weekends and late at night, the princess even tried to make a bacon sandwich. Once, she rang me in a panic at the Old Barracks. 'What's the matter, Your Royal Highness? What's happened?'

'I think the whole place is going to blow up! I can smell gas!' she said.

It transpired that, after making a bacon sandwich, she had left the gas on. 'For heaven's sake, don't let him light a cigarette for a while!' I told her. She opened all of the windows and disaster was averted. Only the princess could almost set the place ablaze by making a bacon sandwich!

Sundays became days off for me. I had never known such a thing. After I had ensured that breakfast had been served and everything was okay, I was allowed home. I had the chance to be with my family, and the princess was free in her home with no one else around to bother her—to bother them.

The chef, who lived away from KP, was also given weekends off, and the princess revelled in the freedom to be mistress and hostess in her home. The boss was never renowned for her culinary skills but she started making simple meals for two: cheese on toast, beans on toast, omelettes and pasta. She used the microwave, rather than the

118

oven, and loved rustling up what she called 'a BJP'—a Baked Jacket Potato. And, of course, there was Kentucky Fried Chicken and, sometimes, take-out samosas and spring rolls when she couldn't be bothered to 'cook'. The chef could also be asked to prepare meals for the weekend, wrap them in clingfilm and leave them in the fridge, American-sized helpings to be split between two.

I was grateful for the break because Monday mornings always meant a 4 a.m. start because I had to go to the market to buy £200 worth of flowers to fill Apartments 8 and 9, including the five window-boxes outside; three outside the drawing room, two outside the sitting room. In the box outside the kitchen window, I planted rosemary, mint, thyme and parsley—for the chef and the boss. The boss loved nothing more than to fling open the Georgian sash windows in the sitting room to let in the sunshine, the fresh air and the perfume from the flowers. Throughout spring and summer, I often went upstairs and found her in the window-seat, enjoying the scent, but never on Monday mornings because she was always up early to go to the gym at the Chelsea Harbour Club, already dressed in Lycra shorts. She'd grab an instant coffee or some orange juice then dash for the stairs. 'Got lots to tell you later!' she'd call.

I knew that the 'lots' would centre on her Sunday with Hasnat, and there were always tell-tale signs of their 'normal' time spent together: washed-up pans and dishes left to drain in the kitchen. Two plates, two mugs, two glasses. I'd wait until she returned for breakfast to be regaled with what they had done, what he had said and how it had made

119

her feel.

Some mornings, her guest was still present at KP, and could be left unattended when the princess had to attend an official engagement or go to a lunch. This gave me palpitations because the importance of remaining 'hidden' seemed lost on him. He forgot that people could see through windows or that maids might pop up in corridors. I preferred it, and was less on edge, when the boss was with him because she obsessed as much as I did about keeping doors shut, and him on a short leash.

It was a strain on the household and the couple that the relationship had to be conducted in such secrecy. It was a clandestine love, treated like a shameful affair, yet the princess was single and joyously in love. I think it opened the man's eyes to the intense fame that surrounded her. In time, that would become an issue that wedged itself between them. But before then they had fun in each other's company, and went to elaborate lengths to go on dates around London.

*　　　*　　　*

I was sent into town with a specific shopping list from the boss: a shoulder-length, straight brunette wig from Selfridges, and a pair of large, round-rimmed spectacles, with clear-glass lenses, from an optician in Kensington High Street. When I returned to KP, she couldn't wait to try them on with a black Puffa jacket and her jeans.

I was in my pantry when I heard her skipping down the stairs. Then she appeared, showing off her new look. She tried to strike a pose with a straight face as I gawped. 'Look at you!' I exclaimed, and the boss's shriek of laughter emerged from behind the stranger's face. She just couldn't stop laughing, holding on to the door frame for support as tears rolled down her face. 'Nobody's going to recognize you!' I said.

This was her disguise to go out on a date with Hasnat, a chance to be anonymous in London.

That evening, they went out as a couple, the princess in her wig and glasses. It was probably the first time since 1981 that she had stepped out in public and not been pursued by the *paparazzi*. She was ecstatic at the glorious freedom of becoming a 'nobody'. I have told of her visit to Ronnie Scott's jazz club previously, but never before revealed that it was to go on a 'normal' date with Hasnat. The couple joined a queue outside Ronnie Scott's jazz club, and the next morning she couldn't wait to tell me all, over breakfast, free of her brunette hair and spectacles.

It has been suggested by others that the boss had a collection of wigs. She did not. She only ever had that brunette one. But the dressing up and disguises didn't last long because Hasnat made a valid and sad point about those special dates. She wasn't allowed to be herself, to be the woman he had fallen in love with. He didn't want to go out with a brunette, bespectacled woman who had to hide her beauty. He wanted to look at the Diana he knew, all blonde hair and blue eyes. The wig, scarves and glasses were discarded because of his reservations. The artificiality had become too much. When the 'fun' of the novelty had worn thin, their dates were restricted once again to KP, his flat or another family home.

121

But even though their relationship was so confined, the rooms at KP were filled with laughter, music and chat. Away from the cameras, with nothing to prove and no 'messages' to send, they were blissfully happy in their own space and company. No yachts, no toys, no helicopters, and no extravagant purchases. This was the *real* thing.

One evening, as she sat up late at her writing desk, she wrote out a poem for him, dipping her fountain pen into the Quink bottle. I hope she had the courage to send it to him. That night, before I left for home, she let me read the verse. It was 'Cloths of Heaven' by William Butler Yeats which seemed to sum up what she felt:

> Had I the heavens' embroidered cloths,
> Enwrought with golden and silver light,
> The blue and the dim and the dark cloths
> Of night and light and the half-light,
> I would spread the cloths under your feet:
> But I, being poor, have only my dreams;
> I have spread my dreams under your feet;
> Tread softly because you tread on my dreams.

*　　　*　　　*

The princess could disappear from KP to spend whole days in his one-bedroom flat, and the joy she derived from those occasions was immeasurable. Diana, Princess of Wales, would return to the luxury of Apartments 8 and 9, sit down with a glass of carrot juice and start to talk, as if she was an ordinary woman from middle England, about how she had spent the day in a poky, sparsely decorated

122

flat, vacumming, polishing, dusting, doing the dishes, ironing piles of laundry, stripping and re-making his bed. She craved such normality, such ordinariness, such self-sufficiency away from the trappings of royalty that had both defined and stifled her.

'I don't mind ironing shirts,' she said. 'It reminds me of when I used to look after an American family and washed and ironed all theirs.'

It transported her back to the days when, as an agency nanny, she had found work with Americans living in London—a job she juggled with her role at the Young England kindergarten in Pimlico, a private pre-school where she was a nursery assistant and drove around the capital in her Volkswagen Golf GTi. Then she dated her 'officer and a gentleman' boyfriend Rory Scott and, every weekend, ironed his shirts. A life so ordinary was repeating itself with Hasnat.

She mentioned how she had gone to his 'bachelor pad' and found days' worth of pots, pans, plates and cups stacked in the kitchen sink, not to mention empty KFC boxes on the counter-tops. I asked her how she had reacted to that, expecting her to frown, but she told me how she had put on a pair of yellow Marigolds and set about tackling the crockery mountain. Once more, history repeated itself.

Friends have recalled how in those days at the kindergarten she donned Marigolds to help out in the kitchen there. Even at Balmoral she was known to find a pair of rubber gloves and muck in with someone else not averse to washing-up—Her Majesty the Queen. The princess would join her mother-in-law at the sink in the log cabin in the

123

estate's grounds to wash up after a summer barbecue.

Whether she was at the kitchen sink or in front of an ironing-board, the boss embraced domesticity with gusto—in much the same way that she embraced Hasnat's family. In the summer of 1996, his grandmother was invited to tea at KP, and presented with a silver dish engraved 'With much love, from Diana x'. She sent me out to Mothercare in Oxford Street to buy the latest double-buggy for his uncle, whose wife had given birth to twins; I had to root out all the boss's maternity clothes, worn when she was pregnant with Harry, so that they could be lent. Both that year and in 1997, the boss took time out of her schedule to spend time with his family at their home in Pakistan—she went out of her way to gain their acceptance and met them all: mother, grandmother, aunts, uncles, nieces and nephews.

When she returned to KP, she was giddy with delight. 'They took me to their hearts, Paul! I had a wonderful time,' she said. She had wanted their approval, and it was crucial to what she had long had in mind.

*   *   *

It was around December 1996 when she said it. And, unlike most things, I hadn't seen it coming.

'This is the man I want to marry,' she declared one evening, curled up on the sofa in her sitting room. She was wearing a jumper and trousers. Her smile expressed pure happiness.

Then she added the words: 'Do you think it would be possible for me to marry in secret with

124

just a couple of witnesses?'

I was waiting for her comedy pause, for her to fall about laughing because it was a joke intended to shock. But she was waiting for an answer, as serious as she had ever been. I knew her relationship with Hasnat was important but it had been only a matter of weeks since the divorce had been finalized. It is significant to point out that whenever the boss was asked by friends about Dodi Al Fayed, she said she 'needed another marriage like a bad rash', but, a year earlier, with the *right* man, she had had no such doubts: she was eager to enter into a fresh union.

Her question to me may sound as though it was meant hypothetically but the princess would never have aired such a thought without first analysing it in her own mind. Therefore, I knew it was loaded with a built-in duty: for me to explore that very possibility.

I was stunned and only hope my eyes didn't give away my surprise. 'I'm not sure what the official protocol would be,' I said, 'but I do know someone I could sound out discreetly.'

The Burrell family priest, Father Tony Parsons, had sprung immediately to mind. He was young, approachable and completely trustworthy.

'Would you, Paul? Thank you,' she said. And that was that: another duty considered done.

I did everything I could to ensure that her life was as complete, happy and easy as possible. Many people outside royal service dismiss a servant's life as some kind of obsequious oddity. I don't know what it was that consumed me in the execution of my duties to Diana, Princess of Wales, but consume me is exactly what it did. Very few people in a lifetime will meet another person whom they would serve to the ends of the earth, and I don't make that statement lightly. But how *can* anyone understand the total, unswerving commitment to another, especially if that person *isn't* your partner? Her reliance on me, and the trust she placed in me, became an addictive force, but it created also an inexplicable, unconditional devotion in me. More than anything, I believed in her. One hundred per cent. It was as plain, simple and complex as that. Just like the simplicity of her request about a secret marriage.

She wanted to marry Hasnat. I'd go as far to say that she had set her heart on it. She wanted to have children with him, and she was prepared to give up everything for him. Even if she didn't realize that giving up her fame would never be possible.

At that time, my son Alexander was an altar boy at the Carmelite church on Kensington Church Street, and that was where I headed the next day to sound out Father Tony. What better person to respect my trust than a Roman Catholic priest? We had an extraordinary conversation sitting in the pews of an empty church. We spoke in whispers which summed up the secret nature of the matter under discussion.

I remember treading carefully at first, asking whether it would be possible for *anyone* to be married in private without the outside world knowing. He told me that it was impossible to perform a marriage service without notifying the proper authorities. 'Why do you ask Paul?' That was when I told him.

He looked aghast. 'It's impossible, Paul! Impossible! It could never be done.'

So, I was the bearer of bad news on my return to KP. The princess was disappointed but understanding, and dismissed all thought and future talk, at least to me, on the subject. But it wasn't going to affect the one thing she was sure about—her future with Hasnat.

*   *   *

'Why don't you go out for a drink?' The princess smiled.

I was quite enjoying the presence of Hasnat in KP because it led, more and more, to boozy nights off duty. When the princess 'treated' me in that way, we both knew what she was *really* saying: she expected me to go for a drink with him and have a man-to-man discussion, sound him out, see what he said, determine what he was thinking. Then I could report back with insight and reassurance. I was the platonic friend who acted as go-between. And I'd enjoy a few pints of Guinness along the way.

The meeting point was always the Anglesea Arms in SW7, between Old Brompton Road and the Fulham Road. We'd sit outside on summer's evenings at the wooden picnic benches, joking about what *Daily Mail* gossip columnist Nigel Dempster would have thought if he'd known what the two men sitting just a stone's throw from his front door were saying. We'd sit there, looking across the road at his Georgian terraced house, and say: 'If only he knew!'

But that observation was an important point to my drinking partner: it was that very anonymity, that we could sit there unnoticed, he wanted so fiercely to protect. We'd always be there at last orders, with me balancing the guilt of returning home late to Maria with the sense of duty that I was acting on behalf of the boss. Besides, I enjoyed Hasnat's company and we developed a friendship that ran parallel to their relationship. Despite the fact that I've now chosen to celebrate that love story, in order to banish the Dodi myth, I know— and he'll know—the mass of secrets that we still share. He knows what we spoke about, what her messages said, the experiences they shared, the places they visited, the future they spoke about and the secrets they entrusted to me. In painting an accurate record of history, I have breached none of that confidence.

The next morning, at breakfast, the princess couldn't wait to hear how the evening had gone. 'Tell me, tell me! What did he say?' she'd ask.

It was at those moments that I switched from being the butler who stood at the sideboard, manning the coffee pot, to the confidant with lots to impart. I'd pull out a bamboo chair, sit down and tell her about it, from start to finish, as she leaned forward, hanging on my every word.

*   *   *

By May 1997, the princess had reached a point where she didn't want to hide him any longer. She was proud—and ready—to allow the relationship to be known publicly. And she knew how to go about it: she would set up a photo opportunity of them together. It would not be an official, posed picture but it would be taken with her full knowledge, by a photographer she trusted, yet it

128

I can see the boss sitting, knees tucked together, on the carpeted step, scribbling down words and thoughts onto her memo pad. It was on these stairs that she sat with me, discussing or composing a piece of correspondence beneath the portrait by Nelson Shanks, (below), see pages 13–14, 250–251.

The drawing room, with its tapestry dominating one wall, was where the boss met her guests; 'the holding area'. Notice the Steinway grand piano between the sash windows. It was from the doorway that I often caught—and watched without her even noticing me—the princess playing Rachmaninov's Piano Concerto No. 2, head back, eyes closed, fingers dancing across the keys.

The dining room, where I best remember the boss sitting at the breakfast table in her white towelling robe, tucking into her grapefruit or twirling a spoonful of honey in her mouth while scanning the morning newspapers . . . sometimes with a towel wrapped into a turban around her wet hair.

The sitting room—the heart and soul of her 'home', where she spent more time than any other room. One abiding memory is the image of the boss sitting at her desk where, at her feet, sat the cuddly hippo. When her work was done, she'd leave her desk and lean against this hippo to watch movies and soap operas on the television, which was stored on an extendable arm within the white cabinet.

It was at her desk that she spent an inordinate amount of time; notice the 'vocabulary list' propped against the letter rack. When she went to France and never returned in August 1997, she had ensured that her desk was neat and tidy. This is exactly how she had left it.

The vestibule lobby at apartments 8 and 9. Through the archway to the left (above) is the hallway leading to the front door; the white door at the other side of the lobby (below) leads directly onto the main staircase. This is the lobby where I said my own farewell to the princess on the eve of her funeral, holding an all-night vigil beside her coffin: a room lit with dozens of candles and filled with the scent of flowers.

The princess's treasured collection of teddy bears and cuddly toys that filled one sofa in her bedroom. Each bear and toy tells its own story.

The dressing room—the inner sanctum very few people ever saw—where the boss would sit in her robe in the bamboo chair, facing the mirror, having her hair blow-dried. This is a memory of a princess at home, when she had removed the mask of royalty and fame. But what I'll never forget is the wall-to-wall images of William and Harry that surrounded her.

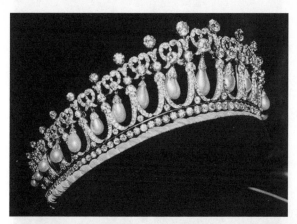

Left The pearl-drop Lovers' Knot tiara—created by Queen Mary in 1914, and worn by Diana, Princess of Wales, on state occasions.

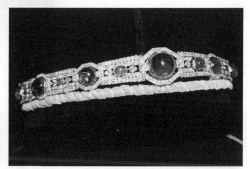

Above and left The emerald and diamond choker which the princess would sometimes wear as a headband.

Below The sapphire and diamond brooch which the boss turned into a choker.

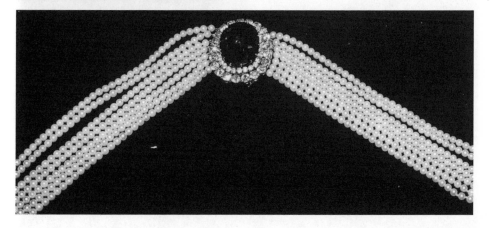

Right The one piece of jewellery that was too precious to wear—the charm bracelet from Prince Charles which includes a gold W and H. This was the most sentimental and important item of her 'crown jewels'.

Below Out and about on the Highgrove estate with Prince Harry and my son, Nick.

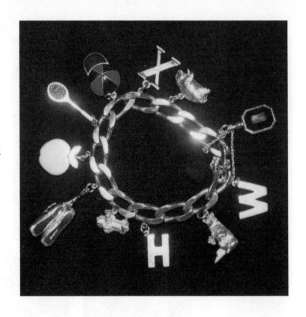

Above A KP family day out at Alton Towers with our 'leader' at the front of the pack.

Below 'Can we go on the giant teacups, princess?'—my sons join the boss and her boys on one of the more gentle rides at Alton Towers.

Travelling abroad with the princess. I took this photo on a tour of Egypt.

Left The sisterhood between the princess and Fergie—it should be remembered for its laughter and happy memories.

Above The princess was inspired by Mother Teresa to pursue a humanitarian path; it was a life-changing friendship for the boss.

behavior is completely directed by external forces totally beyond his or her control. As might be imagined, neurotics, compared with character-disordered people, are easy to work with in psychotherapy because they assume responsibility for their difficulties and therefore see themselves as having problems. Those with character disorders are much more difficult, if not impossible, to work with because they don't see themselves as the source of their problems; they see the world rather than themselves as being in need of change and therefore fail to recognize the necessity for self-examination. In actuality, many individuals have both a neurosis and a character disorder and are referred to as "character neurotics," indicating that in some areas of their lives they are guilt-ridden by virtue of having assumed responsibility that is not really theirs, while in other areas of their lives they fail to take realistic responsibility for themselves. Fortunately,

Above and below Pages marked by the princess's own hand: she underlined and highlighted sections of *The Road Less Travelled* during her journey of self-discovery. She gave me her copy following my mum's death in 1995.

so much that they fear the risk of committing themselves as that they basically do not understand what commitment is all about. Because their parents failed to commit themselves to them as children in any meaningful way, they grew up without experience of commitment. Commitment for them represents an abstract beyond their ken, a phenomenon of which they cannot fully conceive. Neurotics, on the other hand, are generally aware of the nature of commitment but are frequently paralyzed by the fear of it. Usually their experience of early childhood was one in which their parents were sufficiently committed to them for them to form a commitment to their parents in return. Subsequently, however, a cessation of parental love through death, abandonment or chronic rejection, has the effect of making the child's unrequited commitment an experience of intolerable pain. New commitments, then, are naturally dreaded. Such injuries can

Had I the heaven's
embroidered cloths,
enwrought with golden
& silver light,
The blue & the dim & the
dark cloths of night &
light & the half-light,
I would spread the cloths
under your feet:
But I, being poor, have
only my dreams:
I have spread my dreams

under your feet;
Tread softly because you
tread on my dreams.

————.

under your feet;

Some of the
'Wisdoms from
Kensington',
which the princess
shared with me
and many other
friends.

There are many who love God
... they roam the deserts in their
search ... but I will love what
person who loves all of God's
humanity ———.

Iqbal.

Balancing is a
discipline because the
act of giving something
up is painful.....

Above William and Harry were her life.

Below 'Look how much you are loved'—the garden of remembrance laid by the public at the gates of KP in 1997.

would appear, when published in the newspapers, that she had been caught out by a *paparazzi*. The boss was clever when it came to the manipulation of the press, and this was her way of 'handling and controlling' the situation. It remains to this day a subtle practice carried out by many celebrities, agents and publicists as they attempt to control an image. They will agree when and where a picture is to be taken, and usually there will be a hidden motive.

The princess was taking charge of her own PR machine. And her underlying motive? To inform the world that she was in love and blissfully happy. Once his name was in the open, there would be no going back, she said. She had decided to go official.

She had planned on using a trusted go-between in her *Daily Mail* journalist friend Richard Kay. He would *have* to be involved, she insisted, and she was going to seek his advice. She trusted the guidance of the one true friend she had in Fleet Street. She could not have been more enthusiastic or convinced that this was the way forward.

But when her master plan was suggested to Hasnat, his reaction was not what she had expected. He thought it a bad idea, and told her so. He flinched from the spotlight quicker than Dracula ran from daybreak. He was intensely private, and he worried that exposure, with the unwanted fame attached to it, might destroy everything he had worked all his life to achieve. His greatest achievement, as he told me, was what he had made of his life, and he was brilliant in his field. Unlike Prince Philip, who had given up his life and career in the Navy for the Queen, he was not prepared to risk damaging his career, let alone sacrificing it.

'I'm just not ready for it,' he told me one day, over a pint of Guinness at the Anglesea Arms. 'I don't even know if I'm in this too deep,' he added. He dug in his heels.

This man was as stubborn as the boss could be, and he wasn't going to be steamrollered into something that made him feel uncomfortable. His obstinacy infuriated the princess: she didn't like seeing the reflection in him of her own difficult trait. More significantly, I feel she misinterpreted his reluctance as rejection, as a sign that he wasn't ready to be seen with her, that he was unsure about the relationship. In her eyes, if they were happy and in love, it should be shouted from the rooftops.

When he asked for time to think about the photo opportunity, and voiced his doubts, she returned indignant to KP. 'I've had it with him!' she said, and stood in the middle of the sitting room to tell me all that had happened.

It wasn't their first disagreement—there had been periods of silence on both sides before. It's not necessary to explore rows between couples, but the issue of the photo opportunity led to great difficulties between the princess and Hasnat over the following weeks. It refused to go away, and became rooted in intransigence.

If this man didn't understand that to be with her meant being photographed, if he couldn't give way to the introduction of that inevitability into her life and make that sacrifice, then *why* was she making such an effort? Her heart was set on marriage, and his head was making him back away. Or, at least,

146

that was how she saw it. 'I've bent over backwards for him and his family, and this is how he repays me!' she seethed.

It led to a difficult and strained month of June and matters came to a head in the first week of July 1997.

She arranged to meet Hasnat in Vauxhall Gardens, on neutral territory, in the open, at night when it was dark. It had been a warm evening, and it was around ten o'clock. I suppose he should have guessed that the omens weren't good.

They drove there separately, parked and walked to an agreed spot, which was dimly lit. The relationship was to end as clandestinely as it had been conducted. It has long been reported that Hasnat ended it. The truth is that the princess did. She ended it harshly, and in tears, as they stood there in the middle of that London park.

The following morning over breakfast, all I could do was listen as the previous evening's events unfolded, and she explained what had happened, what she had said and how he had reacted. Her hurt and anger had subsided, and she was reflecting over whether she had done the right thing. 'Do you think he'll ring me?' she asked, and I knew then that she had acted rashly, and was partly regretting her emotional impulses.

I offered to take him a message but, on this occasion, she refused. She had chased him too many times, she said.

'He'll come round,' she told me. But he never did, and neither did she relent. Within days, she was on the *Jonikal*.

However, Hasnat did visit KP—without her knowledge—that morning when he knew she was

147

out. He had rung me to check. We sat down, and I witnessed his heartbreak; he had been reduced to tears and to sitting in my pantry. He'd had difficulty in finding a way forward with the relationship but I'm not sure that he'd seen the end coming. Nor, in my opinion, did the princess believe that there was no way back.

A newly single boss wasn't going to sit and mope at KP. Not a day passed without her arriving home and asking: 'Has he rung?' but the answer was always negative. Hasnat had specifically asked me not to mention his visit, and I kept my word. And how I have beaten myself up for that discretion ever since. In the same way the boss regretted, I think, the games she played.

In June—when relations were strained—she had decided to go on an innocent date with Indian businessman Gulu Lalvani, with whom she had been out to dinner with on a handful of occasions. When I noticed that he had driven himself to the front of KP, minus Lawrence his chauffeur, I turned to the princess and said, 'This looks like trouble to me.'

She smiled, as if to say she knew what she was doing and that everything would be fine. To her it was a harmless dinner and a few drinks.

But trouble *was* around the corner. The *paparazzi* snapped her leaving the Mayfair nightclub Annabel's. The pictures were taken at 2 a.m.—pictures that were sure to send a message to Hasnat: that if he wouldn't be photographed with her in public, others didn't seem to mind. She was, I thought, playing a foolhardy game, and I told her so.

Even she wondered when those images made it

into the tabloids. 'What do you think his reaction will be?' she asked over breakfast, knowing that he would be seeing those pictures. And just as she had wanted him to feel proud of her in the newspapers, now she wanted him to be turning green with jealousy.

Rightly or wrongly, it was her way of making him sit up, take note and realize what he could lose. It was a method she would repeat that summer with her public displays of affection towards Dodi.

The idea that she could fall out of love with Hasnat, then fall in love with the Harrods heir is an impossible notion for someone as vulnerable as she was. Everything she did was designed to hit home with Hasnat. She wanted to see that he *was* jealous, that he *did* care, that he *realized* his mistake, and then he'd be back. On *her* terms, not his.

She wouldn't be the first woman to provoke jealousy in the hope of achieving a particular result. Nor would she be the last to realize the futility of such a strategy. I think, in time, she understood that it was hopeless. I think Hasnat felt he had been pushed into an intolerable situation from which there was no obvious way back.

The phone stayed silent, no letters were received and there were no messages for me to deliver. After his secret visit, even he and I lost contact. Two people had allowed something magical to fall apart, and had retreated with their diametrically opposed views on who and what was to blame. They failed to communicate and reach out to each other, and the princess was filled with sadness. It was then that Dodi came along, filling a void with his spontaneous sense of fun, but unable to fill

149

Hasnat's shoes.

I have no doubt that, come the end of August 1997, the boss and Hasnat still loved each other. Who knows what would have happened had the boss returned from Paris? What *has* happened— and this is the travesty—is that the memory of Diana, Princess of Wales, is now interwoven with that of Dodi; the escape she no doubt enjoyed in the Mediterranean sun has become misinterpreted as a 'forever'.

Women across the world know how it feels to emerge bruised from a serious, long-term relationship. The next intimate association they experience is invariably short-lived and no more than a catalyst to help them get over the lost love. That, I'm sure, is what Dodi was to the princess.

In the days after the tragedy in Paris, the only man I could think about was Hasnat, and what he must have been going through in silence as the myth grew legs that 'Diana was at her happiest when she died'.

I didn't know whether to contact him or leave him alone. Then, I received the one phone call that mattered; the phone call, ironically, for which the princess had waited throughout that summer.

'I need to see you, Paul,' he said on the phone. He was in a place where there was no help, no words of comfort. 'I could have saved her,' he said. 'I *could* have saved her!'

I knew exactly what he meant. This brilliant heart surgeon truly felt that had he been on the scene at that car crash in Paris, he not only *could* but *would* have saved her. He said he knew the exact procedure to save a life threatened by a ruptured aorta. 'I could have saved her . . .' he kept repeating.

I told him what I'd learned in the Paris hospital, and what the surgeons had said. He pressed me for details—*needing* to know more of what the doctors had done, how they had explained certain procedures. He was viewing her death through a surgeon's eyes, absorbing and analysing every detail. And as he did so, he became more and more upset that the car crash had happened in Paris, and not London.

'Why did she have to be so far away?' he said. 'I could have saved her here.'

It is ironic that the one man she truly loved was the one man who believed he could have saved her life. Whatever has been said, and will be said, about surgeons having been unable to do anything for the princess, Hasnat felt he could have done something.

It seemed futile to talk about it any further. She was dead, gone. It was too late. But we could still be there for each other so we arranged to meet, in private.

And it was when we came face-to-face, in that week of mourning, that I would give him something precious—something of the princess.

'BOYS WILL BE BOYS'

'Get me out! Get me out!' cried a young Prince Harry. There was panic in his voice, which was almost muffled, as if it was coming from inside a tin bucket. I walked down the hall, and his shouts got louder. Then I recognized a more familiar sound—the hysterical giggles of my elder son, Alex.

'Hurry up! Get me out! Get me out!' yelled Harry.

The boss was away for the afternoon and only the chef, Mervyn Wycherley and I were at KP, with my sons Alex, Nick, and the two young princes, William and Harry, both on exeat from Ludgrove, a rare weekend at home from boarding-school.

My boys grew up with the princes, and became accustomed to Kensington Palace and Highgrove as privileged childhood playgrounds. As butler, I was used to the sight of the four tearing around the grounds and corridors of both royal residences in my service with the princess, and to feeding four hungry mouths at lunch or dinner.

Even if the young princes weren't there, the boss encouraged my boys to spend time at KP. 'I hate the silence in this home—ring your boys, Paul, and get them to come and play up here,' she would say.

So Alex and Nick would race up, eager to play in the palace, and fill the rooms with laughter and noise. The boss loved nothing more than to hear children having fun, filling the emptiness of Apartments 8 and 9.

That day, it had transpired that all four boys would hide in the food lift that served the kitchen and the upper floors. It was designed to carry heavy boxes of wine and vegetables servicing the back door, the loading bay and each floor in KP. But William and Harry had found another use for it. To them, it became an imaginary mine-shaft where they wiled away hours with Alex and Nick. Two boys would go down to the ground floor to where the shaft was located just inside the back door, and the others would be on the top floor in the nursery. The ground-floor 'miners' squeezed into the lift, cross-legged, just fitting into a space reserved for sacks of potatoes. The boys at the top would press the call button, which illuminated the words 'lift coming'. That day, the lift jammed between floors. Which explained why little Harry was screaming to be let out. He was stuck in the lift, and Mervyn had to rescue him, even though the chef could hardly contain his laughter. 'That'll teach you!' he laughed, as Harry scrambled out in the kitchen, almost in tears.

*   *   *

The princess was a devoted mother, whose love for her children transcended anything else in her life. When I think back to the times she shared not just with William and Harry but with her 'surrogate' children—Alex and Nick—I remember joy, laughter and mischief.

Boys will be boys, whether they're members of the House of Windsor or of a butler's family from Cheshire.

Harry and Nick seemed to play non-stop hide-and-seek in the corridors, at least once a day. Harry always chose the same hiding-place: under the table in the nursery.

'I know exactly where he'll be!' the princess would say as she saw Nick rushing off in search of him. Sometimes she would join in the game, always as 'the seeker'. She'd stalk the hallways and rooms listening for the muffled giggles of our sons, and whenever she found them, she'd grab them—'Gotcha!'—and tickle them into shrieks.

153

It was important that KP felt and sounded like a home, not a royal palace, she said. The children pelted up and down the corridors, shouting, screaming, yelling and giggling. My most vivid memory is of Harry running up and down the hallways with a toy gun, crawling across the carpet like a sniper and pretending to shoot the boss as she sat at her desk. If I came round the corner at the wrong moment, he'd turn his gun on me and I'd play dead. I can hear him now. 'Pow-pow! Pow-pow!'

Most of the time, I couldn't watch the Burrell and the Windsor boys at play. I was busy either in my pantry, with other duties or with the princess, and she was content to leave Alex, William, Nick and Harry to run around. So, the best people to recall life with the young princes and their mother are my sons, now young men themselves. Alex is 21 and a student in America, and Nick is 18 and living at home in Cheshire.

Nick was too young to remember Highgrove. Most of his memories stem from KP:

Dad has always told us to cherish our times at KP. How could I forget growing up at a royal palace with the likes of William and Harry? They haven't stayed in touch with us but they were our friends and we were lucky to know them. I hung around with Harry the most, and we always had a laugh.

I remember playing the Sega Megadrive, and then the PlayStation, when it came out, with Harry. He had a fascination with Lara Croft and the Tomb Raider game. On the first level of that game, the player was chased

154

by wolves and bears. Harry got scared and almost wet himself over that stage. Strangely, we both used to enjoy killing off Lara! We also used to play Sonic the Hedgehog for hours on end. The boys were lucky enough to have two television screens and the princess used to allow us to link up the screens so we could play each other, a sort of split-screen format. The princess wasn't so happy when Harry kept playing with the photocopier, making silly faces on the screen and then pressing 'copy'. She said his lips left smudge marks, and he was ruining the machine. I remember her getting quite mad about that.

She didn't seem bothered about us rolling down the stairs, though, grabbing pillows from the sitting room, sitting on them and bumping down each step. We ended up shooting down those steps at some speed.

'Just be careful, boys!' she said, when Harry banged his head and started crying. But he still went back for more.

We'd also jump all over the couches, taking a run up as fast as we could and leaping over the back. Dad said we'd ruin the springs, and was always telling us to stop but we got away with it when he and the princess were in different rooms.

Harry was my best playmate, and we were always play-fighting or having pillow fights in the sitting room or in the nursery. We'd pin each other down. If I was on top of Harry, the princess would count like a boxing referee and when she reached 'ten', I'd jump off. I'd like to think it was those early days that prepared him for the army!

In the summer, we'd have water fights around the gardens. One time, the princess made a police car go up and down the drive, like a moving target, to see if we could hit it with a water-bomb fired from a catapult. When we got really bored, we'd go to see the policemen near the front door at the police box, wander inside, look at all the cameras and try on the police hats. They were always too big for us, and slid down over our foreheads and covered our eyes. There was also a big mower with a motor on it. If you pressed the button, you'd be off. We used to have lots of fun weaving that round the potted plants in the courtyard. I'm not sure Princess Margaret was that pleased with us at times, though.

Snacks and treats were good up at KP. Me and Harry would raid the biscuit tin. We always had those brown Bourbons and pink wafers. Once, we ate a whole box and Harry complained to his mum that he felt sick. She knew he'd been stuffing his face and had no sympathy for him. The chef would make us peach dessert with lots of sugar on top. To this day, it was the nicest one I've ever tasted.

One of my clearest memories is going to see Riverdance with the princess, and we met the entire cast on an amazing night. I remember getting out of the car and holding her hand, and everyone taking pictures. Inside, me and Harry just took the mickey out of a very drunk lady. Harry called her 'smelly' and I think she heard him. She didn't do anything. She was too drunk to do anything.

Another brilliant day out was the day we were allowed to bunk off school to go bowling with William and Harry. There were perks to having princes as friends! I remember the bodyguards being around us and I asked Dad that night why those men had to be there. He told me it was to protect them, to keep them from danger. I remember thinking 'why would Harry be in any danger?' The risks of their role never dawned on me at that age.

It all seems like a different world now but, like Dad keeps telling us, we've got some unique memories.

Alex was older so his memories are a lot more vivid and go back to those idyllic days at Highgrove as well as KP:

I remember Highgrove being very dark. It always seemed gloomy. The kitchen always smelled of butter and the gas from the lanterns. It was peace and quiet, and boring, although we always found something to do. I don't know why but I vividly remember the security room—it was very dark and the monitors were the only things that gave off light. The room always smelled of baked beans. Me and Harry would be allowed by the police to operate the cameras and move them around.

'Where's Papa? Let's find him!' Harry used to say, scanning all areas of Highgrove. We used to think that the cameras looked like giant machine-guns on posts. We'd stand underneath them and wave, and the police in the security room would turn on the lens wipers to wave back at us.

In the summer, I remember Harry, William, Nick and me riding on the gardener's blue JCB and the green John Deere tractors, pretending to be farmers working the land. Or the four of us would catapult water balloons from the stables at the police cars.

Harry, Nick and I would climb the haystacks in the barns and we would compete to see who could reach the top first. Harry would always win. Nick always came last. I wasn't too keen on heights so I wasn't in a rush to get to the top. I also used to be afraid of going up to William and Harry's tree-house. It had to be the coolest tree-house in England. It was like a tower with a thatched roof and red windows. Harry always pretended it was an army watch-tower. He was 'a soldier' inside, outside, everywhere, always armed with a toy gun.

The boys also had a stable converted into a games room, and there was a ball pit and we'd take a running jump into this lake of plastic balls. The princess dived in, too, now and again.

The best thing about being friends with William was that he had an electric-powered, mini-Aston Martin with two leather seats, working dashboard, headlights and everything. Harry had a remote-controlled NASCAR. We always seemed to benefit from playing with the princes' toys, or getting the same presents as them. Neither Dad nor the princess wanted us to feel left out or different. The princess sent Dad to Harrods to buy Tracy Island from the Thunderbirds set for Harry one Christmas. It was the toy to have at the time, and I remember getting dead jealous when Dad told us what his duty had been that day. Then, on Christmas morning, I unwrapped my own Tracy Island— the princess had made sure he got me one, too.

Kensington Palace was such a place of fun, and it was much lighter and more relaxed. I felt awkward larking around inside Highgrove. I felt more at ease in KP. I remember it for the smell of flowers; the princess loved her flowers. Mum and Dad have a florist's shop in Cheshire today. Sometimes, when I'm there, the smell of lilies takes me back to KP.

I remember the treadmill she had near the wardrobe room. Me and Harry thought running on it would make us run 'super-fast' so we'd use it for a bit and then go sprinting around the grounds of KP, thinking we were Linford Christie. When Harry was pretending to run fast, he was pretending to be a soldier. We'd dress up in camouflage and play army in the grounds, running around making artillery gun and bomb sounds. If he became too noisy and his mum told him off, he'd huff and puff and go to his room or the nursery. But then she'd always go and fetch him, give him a cuddle and he'd be back downstairs, laughing and messing around again. She pandered to

Nick's tantrums, too. Harry and I would get on our bikes, race off and leave Nick behind because he could never keep up with us. So he'd go crying back to the princess and she always found a way of making him feel better. He'd sit on her knee at her desk, and she'd spoil him with sweets. Because he was the baby of the four, she had a soft spot for him. He'd always go running to her when Harry and I pretended to be WWF wrestlers, using the princess's expensive cushions as our canvas. Harry was always 'Hulk Hogan', I was 'Bret the Hitman', and little Nick was whoever we said he was.

Nick remembers the snacks and biscuits. I remember the junk food we'd all have, pizzas, burgers, chips and fishfingers, and William and Harry had crumpets for breakfast. They were unforgettable days. My childhood is a continual memory of fun with the princes, and the princess's kindness and hospitality. Nick and I had a lucky childhood when you think about it.

*   *   *

I was there with Prince William when he gave his first speech at the age of ten. His mother didn't want him cursed by the same shyness and lack of confidence that had so blighted her childhood. She wanted to instill self-belief in him; it was part of her grooming process for a future that would see him, one day, become King William V. It was Christmas 1992 when he addressed the annual festive party for staff and tradesmen at KP. Earlier, without the knowledge of his father, the boss had taken her son into the sitting room, encouraging him as he wrote his speech on her pink notepad. The princess was oh-so-proud of him—she talked about that moment all the way into 1993.

She never forgot his first public appearance either, at eight years old. On that momentous occasion, she felt he should appear on St David's Day at Llandaff Cathedral, South Wales, to meet and greet the people of the principality. Side by side, mother and son collected from the crowd dozens of daffodils: the national flower of Wales. She was steering him towards his destiny.

*   *   *

A favourite picture reminds me of 'family KP', and a special day out alongside the boss. Taken in April 1994, it shows the princess, in a green and white New York Jets American-football jacket, sitting cross-legged on a grassy mount, with her sunglasses pushed back into her hair, on a sunny day at Alton Towers theme park. William, Harry, Alex and Nick are standing round her with the rest of the palace household, including Maria and me. Among that twelve-strong group, there was nanny Olga Powell, chauffeur Steve Davies, and two protection officers.

We had travelled from London to Staffordshire by train, sitting *en masse* at one end of an ordinary carriage, the rest of the passengers astonished that the Princess of Wales and her two sons were in standard class, choosing sandwiches and drinks from the refreshment trolley like anyone else.

William and Harry persuaded me to join them on the scariest rides—from the Pirate Ship to Nemesis. I remember screaming with them, as tears of laughter rolled down my cheeks. 'Again! Again! Again!' the young princes would cry. My two boys would be waiting on the sidelines with the boss and Maria, all four too scared to try the white-knuckle experience. For them, something more sedate lay in store.

For young Nick pestered the princess all day long, tugging at her sleeve and jacket. 'Can we go on the giant teacups, Princess? Can we? Can we?' he kept asking.

'I promise you, Nick, we'll do the teacups,' the princess told him.

Not that it stopped him asking every ten minutes. At the end of the day, we gave in and the giant teacups became our last 'thrill' of the day. Nick never left the boss's side that afternoon, always holding her hand, having a piggyback or being lifted on to her shoulders.

The sad thing is that he cannot recall being carried around by the boss. He has seen the photographs but doesn't remember it because he was too young. His only memory is of being in the teacup with the princess, William, Harry and Alex, spinning around. 'Faster! Faster! Faster!' he said.

'No! You're going to make me sick!' cried the boss, who couldn't stop giggling.

That photograph was taken at the end of an unforgettable day.

*   *   *

William and Harry were both expressive boys with

good manners. They were also inseparable and seemed to do everything together. Even to this day, I think it is evident how close they are; two brothers who are always there for one another; two princes who will, I hope, continue to bring warmth, humility and an earthy quality to the House of Windsor. When people ask about the real legacy of Diana, Princess of Wales, they need look no further than her two boys. 'Ma boys!' she used to call them. Never '*my* boys', always 'Ma boys!'

We were under strict instructions at Highgrove and KP to call them William and Harry. No mention of 'HRH' or 'Prince'. Just call them by their names, she said. She was determined to ensure that they enjoyed as normal an upbringing as possible within royal life. It was for that reason that, from their birth, she wanted her hand predominantly to rock the cradle, not that of a nanny, as was the norm in royal circles. She wanted her boys to grow up warm, tender, tactile and loving, not cold and emotionally awkward. When Prince Charles suggested that his nanny, Mabel Anderson, should look after them, the princess refused. She didn't want an elderly woman with old-fashioned views caring for her children.

The princess's approach to motherhood and nannies was fresh and unconventional by royal standards, which was why she chose Olga Powell as the firm, fair and thoroughly modern nanny. The princess smothered her boys with love and attention, giving them what she felt she had been deprived of in her own childhood. I doubt there were many royal households where a princess could have been seen snuggling up to her boys— one on either side of her—while she leaned back against a cuddly hippo in front of her desk, or sitting in a huddle on the sofa watching television.

The princess would also not allow royal advisers to shape her sons' outlook, views and behaviour. She groomed them for a life of duty in her own way, striving to strike the balance between their role and ordinary life. She was determined to open their eyes to harsh realities, to make them realize how blessed they were, and how they could use their roles to help others. She took them on engagements and visits to meet the homeless, AIDS patients, prostitutes, the poor and the disabled. Those people should never be seen as victims, she drummed into her boys, but as 'survivors and courageous'.

She also encouraged them to contribute to adult conversations with her lunch guests at KP. In private, William was asked for his view of his mother's personal problems. She confided in him—perhaps too much at times. He was a child, but his mother saw him as a wise head on young shoulders, who needed to know, but I felt he became a convenient listening post. In her mind, though, she was making him wise for a modern world. 'We have no secrets,' she used to say, and she told him more as he grew older. As far as she was concerned, William was one of the first men in her life whose advice she could trust, despite his years.

Her sons were her world, and she was a wonderful mother. I think it is through her influence that William and Harry have grown into such shining examples of royal gentlemen who are, today, hugely popular. William was shy. Harry was extrovert. William was painfully self-conscious.

164

Harry couldn't care less what people thought. They were the plus and the minus of the same battery. Indeed, William, as a boy, dreaded becoming king. He loathed the thought of a life of duty scrutinized by a media that he felt had hurt his mother. After all, he had seen her tears.

Harry, meanwhile, felt he could change the world, didn't understand the media and said he'd make a good king—if he didn't make a good soldier first.

If mother and sons shared one quality, it was a wicked sense of humour. The sound of laughter was constant when the boys were at KP, and the princess was always nudging them into mischief. Especially at Windsor Castle and Sandringham, where the Royal Family would spend Christmas and New Year.

I had worked for eleven years as the Queen's senior footman and I knew that the monarch loves to laugh. Almost as much as Diana, Princess of Wales did. So I filled William and Harry's Christmas stockings with jokes and tricks to be executed on unsuspecting senior royals: whoopee cushions to be placed on a chair, white sugar lumps that mutated into a thousand miniature plastic willies when dropped into hot coffee, joke cigarettes that exploded like fireworks when offered to 'Aunt Margo', plastic flies set in fake ice-cubes to be dropped into a royal martini or gin and tonic and plastic dog poo carefully placed on the best carpet at Windsor Castle—and blamed on the corgis. The boss laughed with her sons back at KP when they remembered the mischief they had caused.

On occasion, the boss disintegrated into fits of

giggles at William's expense. I'll never forget the time she bought him a calendar—not of page-three beauties but of grotesquely obese women in bikinis. When she saw his face, and how he blushed, she collapsed with laughter, she told me.

William blushing, Harry sucking his thumb—*always* sucking his thumb—and the princess giggling as she cuddled them when they rushed through the black front door, shouting, 'Mummeeeeee!' They were the snapshots in my head from those magical days at KP.

Towards the end of her life, she was proud of the role she had played throughout her boys' childhood. 'They have both been brought up with enormous love, support and direction,' she said, then added: 'Now it is time to find my happiness ... if I'm fortunate enough.'

HIGH FASHION, CROWN JEWELS

The princess was 'walking the catwalk', imitating the stern pose of a supermodel: lips pursed, shoulders back, and strutting with exaggerated steps. It was September 1996, a month on from her divorce.

She was walking up and down, holding up to herself a flowing, strapless flamenco-inspired ballgown, by Murray Arbeid, with black bodice and red skirt. 'What do you think, Paul?' she asked, barely able to stop herself laughing. One of the world's greatest fashion icons was larking around in the privacy of her own home doing what she called 'my Naomi Campbell', dressed in tight-fitting jeans and a jumper, with the gown pressed to her chest.

She looked more like an emu than a catwalk model, but I think that was the general idea. We had been rifling through rail after rail of evening gowns, organizing a mass clear-out when she launched into that impromptu strut in her flat shoes. She would probably never have cut it as a supermodel. Not that that mattered, because Diana, Princess of Wales was established as the undisputed 'Queen of Fashion' with cover-girl status. She didn't need to tread the catwalks of Paris, Milan and London to make an impact because, for her, every day was a fashion show from the moment she stepped out of the front door and was on parade as an icon of style whose glamour, natural grace and versatility captivated a worldwide media. She set trends for a generation of women.

The dresses she wore became almost as famous as the lady herself. Millions of people around the world have a favourite image of the princess, and it's nearly always a picture taken on the world stage when a mood or sense of occasion was matched by a carefully chosen outfit: her dresses could make as powerful a statement as the woman herself.

And it was the worldwide fascination with such statements that had led princess and butler to the dressers' workroom and the ground-floor wardrobe room on a day in late autumn 1996.

'Come on, I want to show you something,' she had said, beckoning me to follow.

'Just look at all these dresses!' she said, opening the floor-to-ceiling white doors, exposing rail after

167

rail of evening dresses, all sorted into colour zones: black at one end, colours in the middle and white at the far end. She walked down the line, brushing her fingers against each garment, counting them. There were sixty-two.

'I won't be needing all these any more,' she said, 'It's time to sell them.'

The boss was starting the process of transition, shedding her skin before she moved on to a new phase in her life. She had decided to auction her wardrobe and raise money for the AIDS Crisis Trust and the Royal Marsden Hospital Cancer Fund.

She led me to the wardrobe room to help her select the dresses that would go under the hammer the following year at Christie's in Park Avenue, New York. She called her dresses 'old friends' because each one told a story.

I opened each of the wardrobe doors around the L-shaped room, exposing dresses she had worn from 1981 through to the mid-nineties. We stood there, looking at this dream collection of *haute couture*, and wondered where on earth to start.

'Look at this one!' she exclaimed, pulling out the first hanger and holding up a silk tartan dress with black velvet bodice worn for dances at Balmoral. 'Absolutely hideous!' she said. Dress number one had been selected.

She picked out another: a strapless ballgown printed with sprays of pink, blue and yellow roses. 'Ah, my Gone With the Wind dress. Looked more like drawing-room curtains!' Then she picked out an outfit that seemed more suited to a Victorian grandma than the Princess of Wales. 'Horrific! What *was* I thinking?!' It was a black velvet dress with Honiton lace frills at the cuffs and neckline.

We must have stood there, selecting dresses—and remembering the nights on which they had been worn—all afternoon, with a break for a pot of ginger tea. It was like watching someone reminisce as they flicked through a photo album, only this was a princess turning over the pages of her wardrobe.

Sometimes, she'd screw up her face, appalled by her erstwhile lack of taste. Or she'd excitedly recount a memory and giggle, or fall quiet in reflection. It depended on what dress came out, and the significance she attached to it. It was a personal experience I shared with her that day, and I think a cathartic one as she prepared for a new future.

She held out a strapless, pale-blue chiffon dress with a crossover yoke. 'I wore this to the Cannes Film Festival in 1987. I felt like a film star,' she mused. (In 2005, the actress Joely Richardson would wear it at the Golden Globes.)

Then came a strapless dress with a blue chintz print on white, worn in Melbourne, Australia, in 1988 when the Prince and Princess of Wales took to the dance-floor. 'He swirled me round the floor that night!' she smiled.

Then came a pearl-and-sequin-encrusted silk gown and bolero worn for an official visit to Hong Kong in 1989. 'It's my Elvis number,' she said, referring to the raised collar, as designed by Catherine Walker.

She didn't need to describe the next dress she chose—I knew its significance immediately. It was her 'Grace Kelly dress', an evening gown of sheer elegance in which she looked stunning.

As soon as she pulled it out, I wanted her to put it back. That all-white sari-like dress was silk chiffon wrapped to below the waist and draped over one shoulder, embroidered with pearlized sequins and beads around the bodice. But she was being ruthless, as well as sentimental, and out it stayed.

Another firm favourite of mine, which held its own memories for me, was the off-the-shoulder black silk crêpe cocktail dress with ruched bodice by Christina Stambolian, bought off-the-peg.

Now in my eyes that *was* a special dress. It was the one I had personally picked out for her to wear in 1994 on the night that Prince Charles admitted his adultery on television. I had told her she looked a million dollars in it, and advised her to stride out with confidence, to show how strong she was, as she arrived for a gala dinner at the Serpentine Gallery in Hyde Park. That knock-out dress filled the tabloids the next morning, and the *Daily Mirror*'s headline was the most apt: *'TAKE THAT!'* it screamed.

The princess said little as she selected it. It wasn't a good memory for her, and she needed to let go of her past.

The one dress she found hard to let go was a Victor Edelstein strapless dinner dress in oyster satin with a long-sleeved bolero, embroidered with carnations, birds and gold beads. 'I'm not sure about this one. It's my favourite,' she said, and stood for a few minutes contemplating what to do. 'When I put this on,' she said, 'I actually *felt* like a princess.'

She had worn it to a state banquet in France as a guest of President and Madame Mitterrand at the

Élysées Palace, Paris, in 1988. It was with a heavy heart that she finally decided it should go because she'd like to think that 'someone will get married in it one day'. When it came to the auction in New York her reluctance to part with it was clear: that dress was the last lot—No. 80.

Over the coming weeks, the boss asked the opinions of friends and other visitors about what gowns should form the sale: 'Dresses from the Collection of Diana, Princess of Wales'. As it turned out, she didn't have as many as she had anticipated so we threw in a few cocktail dresses to supplement them. 'I can't see anyone complaining,' she said.

In total, there were eighty lots but only seventy-nine dresses. The boss specifically asked that there be no No. 13. Whether you are the Queen or the Princess of Wales, that number is always avoided in royal circles.

Fifty of the seventy-nine dresses were by Catherine Walker, the one designer who, more than anyone, had given the princess her 'signature look', and it was a collection everyone felt proud of when it had been collated. Even Prince William was impressed—eventually. He had been credited as the inspiration behind the auction because a conversation with him had prompted the idea in the first place, she told me.

From that moment on, the princess had ensured that her elder son was heavily involved in the dress-selecting process, and I was at KP when the young William waded in with his contribution. By that stage, I had transferred all of the dresses to two coat-rails on wheels in the boys' sitting room. Prince William stood there and flicked through the hangers purposefully, an adolescent boy revelling in the responsibility.

'Mummy!' he squealed. 'How on *earth* did you ever go outside wearing that?' He pointed to a dress she had worn in the eighties. 'No one's going to bid for it!' he added.

The princess turned to him, pretending to be shocked. Then she said, 'Right, William. For saying that, you can make yourself useful by attaching labels to the hangers. Paul will show you what to do!' and she smiled as her son regretted voicing his opinion.

We were all sitting in a chaotic, makeshift fashion factory, butler, princess and young prince, when we were joined by the creative director at Christie's, Meredith Etherington-Smith. She had been treated, on more than one occasion, to the Naomi Campbell impression.

By now, it was December 1996 and the 'system' was working well. As Meredith, a costume expert, described the dresses, the boss sat down with a pen and blue notepad and acted as secretary, writing down the dress number, its style and designer: 'No. 1 navy tulle, Murray Arbeid; No. 4 emerald green cocktail dress, Victor Edelstein; No. 9 black and silver bodice, Catherine Walker . . .' and so on, until the selection had been whittled down to the eventual seventy-nine. Then she hung each dress on the back of a door and took a Polaroid photo of it. Meanwhile, the butler and Prince William had kept quiet, writing labels and attaching them to hangers.

It was a laborious and, at times, exhausting process. I wouldn't be in a hurry to carry seventy-nine dresses, two at a time, up the stairs from

172

ground to first floor again. 'Come on, Paul, keep up the good work!' I can hear the boss saying, as sweat glued the shirt to my back.

The auction took place at Christie's in New York on the evening of 25 June 1997, five weeks before the princess's death. On a fevered night, the dresses raised a staggering £1.85 million for the chosen charities—the ink-blue *Saturday Night Fever* dress fetching a record-breaking $200,000. The princess didn't attend. Meredith telephoned her with the news of what had happened to her 'old friends', and the boss couldn't believe it. Later she and Meredith celebrated quietly over lunch at KP. I still have the Christie's colour catalogue from that auction; it became a tribute in itself to the style of the boss. So, in one respect, her wardrobe had remained a photo album of memories.

It was fitting that, on the first page of the catalogue, there is a note from her, written on the burgundy-edged Kensington Palace stationery: 'The inspiration for this wonderful sale comes from just one person . . . our son William. Diana— June 1997.' It was printed on a page opposite a striking black-and-white photo of the boss in her 'Elvis number', with her pearl-drop tiara and matching earrings.

*   *   *

By royal standards, the princess's collection of jewels was small, some would say paltry, but she was a princess at one with the people on the street and did not feel comfortable with displays of wealth. Ostentatious she most certainly was not.

But the pearl-drop lover's knot tiara, worn on

state occasions or for official portraits, was the most stunning piece with pearls dropping from diamond-encrusted entwined hearts. I was working as footman to the Queen when this ornamental headwear was hand-picked by Her Majesty ahead of the royal wedding in 1981.

The Queen, with her most trusted servant, Margaret 'Bobo' MacDonald, stood in a private room at Buckingham Palace, and opened the eighteen-foot-high cream-painted wardrobe doors to reveal an enormous safe in which drawer upon drawer revealed jewels that had not seen the light since Queen Mary's day. It was a royal Aladdin's cave; a private collection of tiaras, necklaces, brooches, earrings, bracelets and gems that had been passed down from monarch to monarch. The Queen had previously given the princess an enamelled Fabergé egg that represented a ladybird as a gift for her nineteenth birthday.

The most spectacular pieces of the collection are the tiaras, some of which can be traced back to the Russian royal family. During her reign, the Queen has worn no more than six, but there are many others, which she has never worn.

One of these was the Cambridge lover's knot tiara, designed by Queen Mary in 1914. As she and her aide surveyed the collection, the Queen decided that that particular tiara would be loaned to Lady Diana Spencer, then fiancée to Prince Charles, for life.

After choosing the tiara for the future Queen of England, the two ladies then selected further pieces as wedding gifts: a diamond watch, an emerald and diamond choker, and the bejewelled Family Order, which all royal ladies wear on state occasions—a miniature portrait of Her Majesty set into a gold 'badge' and surrounded by diamonds surmounted with an enamelled crown. Pearl-drop earrings to match the tiara were a gift from Prince Charles. The princess also had use of the Spencer family tiara, lent to her by her father to wear on her wedding day. It remained with her to use for state banquets at Buckingham Palace until her brother, Charles Spencer, demanded its return in 1993, reminding her it had only ever been 'on loan' and 'should now be returned to its proper owner'.

The emerald and diamond choker—which the princess famously wore as a headband during a dance with Prince Charles in Australia in 1985— was steeped in history, having also been created by Queen Mary. It complemented a different tiara; which the Queen decided not to give to the princess. That tiara is now worn by the Duchess of Cornwall. The Delhi Durbar tiara was loaned to her when she finally married Prince Charles in 2005.

The princess was meticulous about looking after her 'crown jewels', keeping each piece in its cushioned presentation box and locked in a modest safe under the stairs at KP. She treasured them as jewels and memories, recording their origin and who had given them to her.

For example, on the inside of the Fabergé egg box, she had pinned a label that read: 'Birthday present from the Queen—July 1st 1981'. The pair of emerald and diamond drop earrings given to her by Prince Charles bore the legend: 'Given by C for my 22nd Birthday'.

And in the presentation box with the tiara, the label proudly declared: 'Tiara given to me by The

Queen as a wedding present'.

Whether the boss was labelling CDs, her favourite books or royal jewels, she had the endearing habit of identifying a possession as hers. But those labels, stuck discreetly inside the jewellery boxes, said much more: they showed how proud she was to be a princess, and to have received such a gift from the Queen. Not from 'Mama' but from 'The Queen'. It was almost as if she couldn't quite believe it.

One other significant piece of jewellery that the princess treasured had been a gift from the Queen Mother. The label read, 'Engagement present given to me by Queen Elizabeth, February 24 1981'.

Inside the box was a huge single sapphire, approximately twenty carats, surrounded by two rows of brilliant-cut diamonds; the outer row larger than the inner. It was meant to be worn as a brooch, and was similar to the brooches Queen Victoria had had made for her daughters. But the princess never wore brooches so she decided to make it the centre-piece of a choker-necklace of seven rows of cultured pearls. Without doubt, it was her favourite piece of jewellery and she famously wore it on the night she danced with President Reagan and John Travolta at the White House.

She never wore the piece of jewellery to which she attached most sentiment, because it was 'too precious'—the charm bracelet given to her by Prince Charles. Each year, for the first ten years of their marriage, he sent her a charm to be added to the gold chain-link bracelet he had also bought her. In 1982 and 1984, he sent her a gold W and an

H to mark the births of their sons, then an X for their tenth wedding anniversary. Other charms he bought her included a pair of ballet shoes, for her love of dance, a tennis racquet, for her favourite sport; a polo cap, to represent his passion, a miniature St Paul's Cathedral for where they were married; a bear, for her love of teddy bears, an apple to represent her love of Manhattan and a pig, which must have been a private joke! That bracelet was always kept in her safe and it was a constant and special reminder of all the good times in her marriage, she said.

I loved assisting the princess in the selection of jewellery for a special occasion. For what turned out to be her last birthday, 1 July 1997, when she was determined to wow 'The One' after attending a gala dinner at the Tate Gallery, designer Jacques Azagury had created a full-length black evening-gown in chantilly lace covered with sequins and beads, and finished with black satin straps and bows. He'd made it as a surprise 36th birthday gift, and had personally delivered it to KP. The boss was bowled over by his generosity.

'You *must* wear it tonight!' I told her, as she paraded up and down in the sitting room, having slipped into it within minutes of its arrival. I dashed across the landing to the safe and pulled out some sapphires and diamonds.

'No, Paul, not those. I want to wear emeralds,' she said, rushing after me.

That night, she wore the dress, and completed the look with the art-deco emerald and diamond bracelet Prince Charles had given her as a wedding gift, the emerald and diamond drop earrings he had also bought her, and Queen Mary's cabochon

177

emerald and diamond choker.

*　　　*　　　*

I always marvelled at the transmogrification from private 'princess at home' to the public 'queen of fashion'. At times, even the boss pondered the dramatic change as she studied her reflection in the mirrored wardrobe doors in her dressing room. She stood there, front on, side on, then a glance over her shoulder, checking every angle. And she always, always touched or tweaked her hair before she rushed for the door. It was habit.

The boss would never have called herself 'a natural beauty'. She didn't consider herself 'beautiful', and that wasn't simply down to low self-esteem. She was just making a realistic assessment when the public gloss was removed. But what she *did* know was that when she pulled it all together— the hair, the makeup, the clothes, the jewels—she looked sensational. Whatever she might have thought privately, the end result was breathtaking beauty. She was a formidable presence, and this was the icon of fashion the world came to know, love and remember.

My memories are somewhat different, though. Where the people on the outside witnessed the 'queen of fashion', I saw the 'princess at home', and watched the transformation in reverse: the removal of the makeup and a face scrubbed clean, the hair tied back with a cloth band, the heels kicked off, the dresses swapped for the white towelling robe, the jewels placed in their boxes. And a mug of coffee clasped in both hands, instead of a champagne flute.

178

At weekends, I was used to her lounging around the house in jeans and jumper. Even if they happened to be Armani and Ralph Lauren. Women are always intrigued by the princess's tastes and sizes. In the UK, America, Australia and Japan, I've told inquisitive females that she stood five feet and eleven inches tall in her stockinged feet; her favoured colours were reds, blues and blacks; her shoe size was a six and a half, usually snug in a pair of Jimmy Choo or Salvatore Ferragamo; she could be a UK dress size ten or twelve, depending on the fit and cut, and much of her eveningwear was strapless because the boss knew she had a good neck and shoulders!

She had a clever knack of mixing royal jewels with costume jewellery. People are often surprised to learn that the Princess of Wales didn't always opt for *real* jewels, and on many an occasion she must have fooled even the most discerning eyes. She could mix and match with the best of them. The boss was like any other modern woman: she could never have enough clothes, enough shoes, enough handbags. She often refreshed her collections, and gave many no-longer-wanted items to friends and staff.

In 1997 fashion writer Suzy Menkes wrote about the boss's style in the *International Herald Tribune*, saying: 'The Princess of Wales may have appeared first as a clothes horse and sometime fashion victim. But as she broke free from constraints, her clothes expressed her independence. In the last years of her brief life, her style became symbolic of post-feminist dressing. The body-conscious clothes, gym-honed figure and confident sexual allure expressed the spirit of her thirtysomething generation, free of bourgeois inhibitions that once filled women's closets.'

And that was why so many women identified with her.

What I remember best about her style is its simplicity and practicality, as worn at KP, not the intricate, pristine look that made her famous. She often padded around the apartments barefoot, and I can still see those feet tucked under her legs as she curled up on the sofa, snug and comfortable, not dressed to impress. Or I would walk into the sitting room and find her perched on her wooden stool with her back to the sofa; one knee bent tight to her chest as she painted her toenails with her favourite colour—noir rouge. Or clutching a hand-held magnifying mirror to pluck her eyebrows that were 'coming through'. And, with the television on or the CD playing, she was forever applying moisturizing cream to her hands and arms, rubbing it in with long sweeping strokes.

*   *   *

The princess put a lot of thought into the dresses she wore, always conscious of being in the public eye, aware that she would be photographed, and never in doubt that a particular outfit would be scrutinized for its style, appropriateness and 'meaning'. The fashion of the princess was as much a matter for public and media debate as her love-life and marriage so she chose each outfit or dress to suit the occasion, whether she was nipping down to the gym or attending a banquet at the palace.

When she wore a Virgin Atlantic sweatshirt to the Chelsea Harbour Club, she knew it was a secret endorsement of the airline, and would have won the approval of its owner, Richard Branson: it was a favour to a friend. On the night she wore the Christina Stambolian cocktail dress, she knew that dress conveyed the message : 'I'm here to stay!', even if it did mask private pain. And on the night of her last birthday, when she wore the black beaded evening gown for Hasnat, she knew it would first dazzle the media—and then wow her man.

But her dresses also illustrated her tact and diplomacy. Over two or three fittings, she would consult and work in close detail with a chosen designer to ensure that the 'message' of a particular dress fitted an occasion. Those were her 'statement dresses'; the dresses that did the talking with one powerful image.

For example, for Saudia Arabia, Catherine Walker designed an ivory satin long-sleeved evening dress embroidered with golden falcons, the symbol of the House of Saud. For Japan, she created a two-piece cream suit edged with red, and a matching hat that bore a significant red symbol—the rising sun.

In Thailand, the boss was whisked around a ballroom in another Catherine Walker sari-style evening-dress in fuschsia pink and purple—the colours of the Thai royal house.

She'd also wear Chanel in Paris, Escada in Germany, Moschino in Italy, khaki trousers to army bases. She *knew* how to make an impression and show respect for the countries she visited without needing to say a word. Her fashion sense came complete with perfect manners.

When I moved to KP, she even ensured that *my*

wardrobe was up to scratch. 'A woman always likes to influence a man's wardrobe,' she joked. If I was to be her shadow then I had to be well-dressed! She preferred me not to wear the traditional butler's uniform, which had been *de rigueur* at Highgrove. Even in that regard, she was rebelling against royal rules for household staff, making sure *her* staff were different and that her household was independent of the House of Windsor.

But the main reason for the change was that in civvies I could be a much more anonymous figure beside her. We went shopping together: the boss was the in-control female in the stores while I was the compliant, under-the-thumb male. It was like your mum taking you to a clothes shop as a kid, kitting you out in what *she* wanted *you* to wear— though my mum never took me to places such as Turnbull & Asser in Jermyn Street, Ralph Lauren in Bond Street, Hermès in Sloane Street and Harrods in Knightsbridge: we didn't have many of those shops in Chesterfield. I walked away with an entire new wardrobe of polo shirts, slacks, shoes and silk ties.

'There we are! *Much* better!' she said, when I did a brief fashion show of my own at KP. I was a little embarrassed that day. I had a new wardrobe, as created by Diana, Princess of Wales, but it was nothing compared to the new wardrobes that came each season for her, courtesy of Gianni Versace.

After he had showcased a new collection on the catwalks of Paris, London and Milan, he despatched the very same collection of evening dresses, day dresses, coats and shoes to KP.

It arrived in giant cardboard wardrobes to the delight of the princess. Each new fashion season

182

was like Christmas, the boss eager to see what treats Versace had in store for her. We then carried arm-fulls of clothes into the wardrobe room on the ground floor. The problem was that many of the items were so 'catwalk', as the boss used to say, that they were either impractical, too daring or not made-to-measure.

Sometimes, because Versace knew her size, an outfit would be perfect, or the dressers at KP could alter something to fit if she found it irresistible. 'I'm so lucky! He's such a generous man!' the princess said when the collections arrived. Versace's generosity lasted until his murder in Miami, in July 1997, just weeks before the princess's tragic death.

The boss had always been fascinated by fashion, even before she was familiar with Versace's work. Long before I knew her, she had grasped its nuances. In 1983, during the Prince and Princess of Wales's royal tour of Canada, she wore an intricate pink and peach silk dress and ribboned hat in the style of the 1880s. It was ruched at the back and sides and had a lace collar, bodice and cuffs. She and her husband, wearing 19th-century formalwear, were attending an event in Fort Edmonton, Alberta, to celebrate the 1898 Klondike gold rush. Later the princess laughed at pictures of this outfit. 'It looks like we're at a fancy-dress party!' she giggled as she rifled through old photographs of that occasion. 'And just look at Charles!'

But the pictures didn't tell half of the story. The dress was the creation of Oscar-winning costume designer John Bright, but it was its history that amused the princess and, in choosing that particular ensemble, she had revealed her mischievous streak. The dress had been worn first by the actress Francesca Annis in the 1978 BBC mini-series *Lillie Langtry*, which was about the life of the British high-society actress turned American citizen who was the 'semi-official' mistress to Queen Victoria's son Albert Edward. Otherwise known as The Prince of Wales. Even more significantly, Lillie Langtry had shared the affections of the prince with Alice Keppel—the great-grandmother to Camilla Parker Bowles. The princess knew all about the story and, at a time in her marriage when, despite being happy, her suspicions were building, she latched cannily on to the significance of the dress. 'I don't think anyone at the palace realized its history,' she winked.

In Canada, that dress remains a famous image. Anne Lambert, professor and curator at the University of Alberta's Clothing and Textiles Collection, has said: 'It moves people because it depicts Charles and Diana at a very happy period of their marriage when they were the fairytale couple.'

*　　　*　　　*

It was Jacques Azagury who encouraged the boss to be more adventurous in the fashion she wore. He had been creating dresses for her since 1989, and also became a good friend to me. I had heard all about him during days at Highgrove when the princess had told me about her visits to his London showroom. Her fittings were in three stages: first, when the dress was skeletal; second when it was almost complete; and third when it needed only to be zipped up.

I'll never forget the time when, after Jacques had zipped the princess into a new dress, she was almost giddy with excitement. 'Paul! Paul! Come and look!' she shouted.

I walked into the sitting room and saw the diminutive figure of Jacques beaming with satisfaction. The boss was wearing a powder blue dress with vermicelli beading and spaghetti straps. Then, for both butler and designer, she launched into her catwalk strut, from one end of the sitting room to the other. 'Isn't it gorgeous?' she said.

That was in 1997 when Jacques was ever-present at KP, helping to replenish the wardrobe that was due to go under the hammer at Christie's.

At least she got to wear some of Jacques' dresses that year. In June of that last summer, she wore a hand-embroidered, blue shift cocktail dress to the Royal Albert Hall for a performance of *Swan Lake* by the English National Ballet, and his scarlet dress with a full skirt and a deep V at the back in Washington on a visit to the National Museum of Women in the Arts, illustrating the daring, seductive yet sophisticated nature of Jacques' designs. He was responsible for encouraging her to wear shorter skirts, to 'show more leg', and after some early resistance the princess took his advice: her hemlines rose by two or three inches. She started to wear heels more often, when previously she would have opted for flat shoes. She was embracing a more risqué sense of fashion for a royal. Jacques was determined to bring out her sex appeal without turning her into a sex symbol.

The boss had stopped dressing to please the 'grey suits' and fulfil expectations of how a princess should dress and began to dress for herself, which, in turn, boosted her self-confidence. The more she 'found' herself in fashion, the more the British public was wowed by her, a princess who was both regal and sexy. The girl who had once been intimated by high fashion was now embracing it, and how she looked mattered hugely to her. I think she analysed her image too much. But the more people encouraged her—be it a designer or her friends at *Vogue*—the more daring the clothes she wore. She often giggled at the discoveries she made about herself with a lower neckline, a higher hemline, a bit of heel, a sleek, figure-hugging dress.

She didn't just remain with British designers. She adored Chanel and Versace, carried handbags by Lana Marks and Christian Dior. Like any woman, she took time and many years to find what suited her and what she liked, then strode out with confidence. What she wore was elegant, sexy and unfussy.

She began to dress more like a Hollywood A-lister than a British princess and no single style 'belonged' to her. The simple fact was that she looked amazing in whatever she wore, and the more daring or form-fitting the outfit, the more impressive she was. Heads turned and jaws hit the floor whenever she stepped out in a new design.

I can't remember too many fashion faux pas in her life. Except, perhaps, in the early days. Her first visit to Balmoral, when she was courting Prince Charles was almost a fashion disaster. Pauline Hillier, a housemaid, was assigned to look after the shy, blonde girl who blushed easily and seemed slightly out of her depth. When Pauline came down to the staff quarters, it was clear that the then Lady Diana Spencer had little idea about dress. 'This is my lady's dress,' said Pauline, holding up a simple black evening dress on a hanger. 'She's only got the one—and she's here for three nights!'

As it turned out, the new lady on the arm of Prince Charles was spared her blushes thanks to the summer weather: the Queen held barbecues on the two other evenings. One evening dress had been just enough.

But that was then, and the boss had long been transformed since those shy, reticent days. Innocence and naïvety had turned into self-assured grace, and she had learned to walk tall and proud. She had ditched the traditional, conventional look of most royal women to become a figure who graced the front cover of *Vogue* rather than *Majesty* magazine; a far cry from the girl we first saw at Balmoral.

In a newspaper article published in July 2006, Jacques Azagury wrote about the changing personality of her fashion: *'I urged her for years to make more of her allure but she was always afraid of drawing criticism from the Royal Family. Her natural instinct was to hide away. I told her, 'You're a beautiful woman—enjoy it! But it took years before she was able to believe that about herself.'*

By 1997, the boss had come to believe him and others, and Jacques wrote: *'I could see that she felt free, unburdened, as if everything which had frightened her or troubled her had all come into focus. She saw it all for what it was and was no longer afraid. There was an unmistakable determination about her, none of her usual uncertainty. She was no longer suffering...'*

He had created one particular design—his best and most daring—just before she went away on holiday with Dodi Al Fayed that August. I was called upstairs from the pantry to offer my male opinion.

'Do you think it's too low?' she asked, raising her eyebrows as my eyes scanned the plunging décolleté which revealed more than usual.

I shook my head emphatically. 'It's perfect!' I replied. Jacques was nodding with approval as we both stood back to admire her in the amazing dress.

I can't begin to describe how stunning she looked, even in that half-made, black silk georgette dress with a split running up to the lower thigh. When it was finished, it twinkled with thousands of bugle beads and had a fish-tail train. She planned to wear it to the film premiere of *Hercules* in October 1997. If ever she had taken delivery of a red-carpet dress, that was the one. It would have sent the *paparazzi* into a spin, and the media would have been falling over themselves to capture the moment, to capture the princess in that dress. We were all excited by it, and she couldn't wait to parade it in public. 'It's a showstopper,' said Jacques, admiring his work.

It was a sign of how far the princess had come, and how her self-confidence had grown, that she 'couldn't wait' to wear it. It would be, Jacques promised, 'the most dazzling, sexy creation you will ever wear in public' because of the split up the thigh and the plunging neckline. In the old days, the boss would have blushed. Now, she stood there and gasped with anticipation, then broke into a fit of excited giggles.

It was the best dress she never got to wear and, while that saddens me, I will never forget her excitement. In a funny way, it remains bottled, fizzing in my mind. And for me, the memory is a privilege because only the butler and the dress designer had a glimpse of how beautiful she would have looked in it.

SISTERHOOD

The boss was at her desk, with a pile of mail to her right, when her attention was drawn to a specific envelope. At first glance, it didn't look out of the ordinary: A4-sized, yellow-brown in colour, and addressed, like most of the others, to 'HRH the Princess of Wales, Kensington Palace, London, W8'. But on closer inspection the princess knew something was amiss. Its flap was Sellotaped flat for extra security, but the handwriting was the spidery, uncertain scrawl of a child; children usually just licked the seal. Inside, she could feel a greetings card of some kind. It might have been a belated birthday wish—she received it in the first week of July 1997, when she had just turned thirty-six.

Then she saw the initial in the bottom left-hand corner of the envelope. This was the give-away clue to its origin because it meant it had been written by a royal hand—a royal child's hand. An initial in the corner of an envelope is a signal used among the Royal Family to tell a recipient that, among the piles of mail, this item is personal. The

Queen always scribbled the initials 'ER', the princess 'D', Prince Charles 'C'. The initial on the envelope in the boss's hand was 'E'.

The princess took her silver letter-opener and slit the envelope open. I returned to my pantry so that she could read the correspondence in private.

As I sat downstairs, the floorboards above me started to creak. And creak. And creak. The boss was pacing, which meant that whatever she was reading, or had just read, had upset her.

It was later that day when the full story emerged. The princess left that envelope propped up in my pantry, and had written on it: 'Paul, when you've read this, please shred it!'

I read it, and immediately understood why she was so angry. What had spilled from that envelope was the dramatic dénouement in the sad demise of a friendship. After a series of difficult episodes between Diana, Princess of Wales, and Sarah, Duchess of York, this piece of correspondence was the last straw in what had been a unique sisterhood, and Fate wouldn't give them time to heal that most unnecessary rift. It was a sad end to a special friendship, and seemed such a waste.

*   *   *

'You jump, and I'll jump,' the sisters-in-law would laugh in agreement. It was a light-hearted pact between the boss and the duchess, their way of saying to one another, 'We're in this together. We face our troubles together. We'll be there for one another.' At least, that was the plan that initially underpinned the royal friendship.

For more than a decade, the two ladies shared

the closest of bonds. They were a sort of royal Thelma and Louise, on the run and rebelling within an institution that smothered their respective ideas of happily-ever-after, and frowned upon their free spirits. 'The Wicked Wives of Windsor' was how Fleet Street began to refer to them, but regardless of what the grey suits of the Royal Household might say, there was nothing wicked about either 'outsider' who had married into the family: they were two kind and loving women with complex characters and profound vulnerabilities, provoked by the cold realities of royal marriage, duty, public scrutiny and a critically judgemental, stuffy Household.

They had known each other since childhood as distant cousins, and started enjoying regular lunch dates from 1982 before the duchess had started dating husband-to-be Prince Andrew. At the outset, though, as in most sisterhoods, sibling envy niggled behind mutual admiration. The boss observed Fergie—as the duchess is known—her carefree manner and natural *joie de vivre,* and wondered why she couldn't be 'more like her'. Even Prince Charles once said, 'I wish you would be like Fergie—all jolly!'

That remark was said in the early days but haunted the boss. Whenever self-doubt crept into our conversations, I tried to reassure her that her personality was just as sparkling but was bound into a much more restrictive straitjacket because she was the future Queen of England. Fergie, as wife to the fourth in line to the throne, had more freedom to operate as she wished. No doubt, that was why her behaviour was often criticized as 'unbecoming in a royal'. There was no escaping that the princess was an introvert, and the duchess an extrovert, and the shy will always look sideways at the confident and force a smile.

But, as with many outwardly confident people, the duchess's public performance was a façade that hid a multitude of insecurities. She, too, was ravaged by self-doubt and low self-esteem, and feared rejection just as much as the princess. 'Why do people say such hurtful things about me all the time?' she would say, contradicting the couldn't-care-less public persona after *The Spectactor* had described her as 'vulgar, vulgar, vulgar' and newspapers had dubbed her 'The Duchess of Pork'.

She would worry about people's motives, what those she met thought of her, and get anxious about 'spooks' conspiring against her. When she talked, her language seemed strewn with references to 'blackness', 'darkness', 'dark sides' and 'bad signs'. She sought refuge in, and reassurances about her future from, psychics in much the same way that the boss relied on astrological readings about the way ahead.

Behind the scenes, the duchess was much more vulnerable and less of a survivor than her sister-in-law. In that respect—and this was something the boss didn't appreciate—the weaker always look sideways at the strong.

I think their differences helped them to prop each other up over the years. Ultimately, it was the princess who shone through. Her personality and decorum in public won her millions of admirers and fans around the world while Fergie bolted recklessly along like a loose horse that had unseated its jockey.

From about 1994 onwards, the boss's doubting comparisons of herself with Fergie subsided and, in the final year of her life, she didn't say anything about wanting to be like her. By then, she had recognized her own sterling qualities and seen the apparent flaws in others.

Nevertheless, before then, her friend's fizzing company had long been a guaranteed pick-me-up. And Fergie's energy seemed limitless. She could bolt up the main staircase faster than a princess in a hurry or a butler with an urgent call to answer. She positively leaped up those stairs—it was like opening the doors to a gale-force wind.

'Hi Paul!' she'd shout, and be off in a flash of red hair, racing up to see her one true friend within the House of Windsor, waiting for her in the sitting room.

For many years, the 'sisters' gossiped and shared secrets, were never off the phone, and when the duchess visited KP, their hilarity always made me smile. Then I'd walk upstairs, going about my duty, and find them engrossed in each other's conversation, rocking on the sofa in fits of giggles. More often than not, though, there were serious heart-to-hearts, shared tears and serious advice. In the main, though, I remember the sisterhood for its laughter and mischievous sense of fun. It was a special friendship that didn't deserve to end the way as it did, in an unhealed rift.

*   *   *

The duchess called the princess 'Duch'. 'Dearest Duch!' she'd say, in an enthusiastic beginning to either a conversation or a letter. The boss had had that nickname in childhood because 'They thought I was quite grand from an early age!' she told me. Only those closest to the princess used it, there were never any airs and graces between the princess and the duchess.

As footman to the Queen from 1976 to 1987, I had a unique perspective on that royal friendship, as I had witnessed both ladies' introduction into the Royal Family. In 1981, when the nineteen-year-old Lady Diana Spencer married Prince Charles, I served the bride's table at the wedding breakfast at Buckingham Palace. In 1986, when a twenty-six-year-old Sarah Ferguson married Prince Andrew, I rode in the ceremonial procession to Westminster Abbey behind Her Majesty on the back of her state landau.

Gradually, albeit formally at first, I had got to know both ladies on their respective visits to royal residences such as Balmoral and Windsor. In June 1987 I snatched a first glimpse of their mischief at my last Royal Ascot shadowing the Queen—I left her to serve the Prince and Princess of Wales at Highgrove that August.

I was in the Royal Box in the grandstand, at the back where tea is served between the third and fourth race. I was looking down on the crowds and the paddock through the windows, pulling the net curtains to one side. It was from that vantage-point that I saw the Royal Family walking through the Royal Enclosure, cutting a swath through the crowds—and spotted the naughty duo of the princess and Fergie, poking an umbrella into the backside of the top-hat-and-tailed Major Hugh Lindsay, the Queen's equerry-in-waiting. (He was killed the following year in an avalanche at

Klosters, Switzerland, while skiing with Prince Charles.) The two ladies were fond of the major: they described him as 'a true star trouper', and as he walked in front of them, they jabbed him with that umbrella, egging one another on. They laughed, and the major did his best not to laugh.

The boss and the duchess were clearly having fun that day with the umbrella because the newspapers captured Fergie jabbing someone else with it. It was their behaviour with the major, witnessed by others, that caused disquiet behind the scenes, though. The Queen thought it 'the most inappropriate behaviour' in public, let alone at Royal Ascot and the pair became the talk of the Queen's box. Even I winced at their behaviour. Within two months, however, when the princess had become my boss, I would witness her humour and mischief at first hand.

Even then, the differences in character between her and the duchess were stark.

In the run-up to her wedding, I'd seen the princess retreat into isolation at Buckingham Palace, lost and shy in its vastness. I saw Fergie embrace married life in the same palace like a little girl let loose in a sweet shop after she had discovered that everything was free. She threw virtual banquets for dozens of friends, sometimes socializing beyond midnight. The princess would eat alone, nibbling a Big Mac; almost too scared to pop her head out of the door of her suite.

It was no wonder that the media described Fergie as bubbly, a breath of fresh air, but when I moved to Highgrove, the simplistic use of labels annoyed me as I drew closer to the boss, and began to understand what made her tick. On one hand there

195

was a shy princess riven with neurosis that had led to an eating disorder caused by a miserable marriage; on the other, there was a bundle of positive, well-balanced joy and happiness in the form of a duchess who broke the mould. Even in those days, the scales were weighted all wrong.

At Highgrove, when the princess started coming into the kitchen for company and chats, we'd talk about Fergie, and it's fair to say that the boss wondered aloud about the public perception of a duchess who appeared so cavalier in comparison to her own considered, more careful approach.

It was on those occasions that I voiced my frustration about the inaccurate media portrayals: for me, the princess was the freshest air to blow through the system, not Fergie. I don't know whether the boss ever questioned Fergie about her approach. All I know is that I continued to open the front door at Highgrove to her, Prince Andrew and the princesses Beatrice and Eugenie who would run around the grounds with the young princes William and Harry. The girls kept the boys entertained while the duchess was a welcome distraction for a princess facing misery and rejection in her own marriage. Fergie and the girls would sometimes stay overnight in one of the two guest suites, favouring the green room with its four-poster bed and views of the front drive and across the paddock towards the spire of Tetbury church. At those times, the house was filled with laughter and the sound of children playing. Even Prince Charles would chase the children round the grounds as the Big Bad Wolf, growling as he came near them. It was the nearest the princess came to playing happy families.

On hot summer days, the royal cousins would trot out on the boys' ponies, Smokey and Bandit, or the princess, the duchess and the children would go down in their swimsuits to the swimming-pool in the corner of the garden beside the stable block. Later, the boss took the boys to Fergie's swimming-pool at her residence, Sunninghill Park, near Ascot. I think I preferred it when the boss was the visitor and not the host: staff at Highgrove—a slick, regimented household running to the strict order of Prince Charles—knew that when Fergie was around, anything could happen. She was spontaneous, unconventional, unpredictable and nearly always running late. Some argued that she was a bad influence on the boss. She tried to pull the boss out of her shell, encourage her to be braver, to socialize more, and often dropped hints that the princess spent 'way too much time in her shell'.

As the duchess wrote in her autobiography, *My Story*, in 1996: 'I knew Diana had very little social life. She never went out, never did anything except be adored.' Aside from beauty and duty, Fergie felt she should live a little more. However well-intentioned the advice, it served only to prompt more self-doubt.

The boss could never see what others saw in her, and never appreciated her own qualities. The slight jealousy she felt towards Fergie, especially because she had a husband who was passionately in love with her, obscured the blindingly obvious: however genuine, charming and down-to-earth Fergie was, she could also be loud and uncouth. And whenever people are overly loud and gregarious, it's normally a pretence of confidence;

197

an over-compensating defence mechanism. The duchess often wore that mask. With the princess, what you saw was what you got, her fragilities and flaws occasionally on display. She was refined, not raw, and displayed quiet confidence, elegance and sophistication. I'm sure the duchess was equally jealous of her—of her beauty, her glamour, her body, and her sympathetic press.

The boss was her friend's guide to life within the Royal Family. With four years' experience under her belt, she virtually lit the path that lay ahead. Whatever mistakes the boss had made, Fergie did the opposite. Whatever successes she had mastered, Fergie copied. Where one had had to find her own way, the other had a lead to follow. And the boss was a giant of a guide: as a whispering adviser at Fergie's first public appearance in 1986, as a listener when married Fergie was disgraced over the toe-sucking affair, as a source of comfort during the ensuing breakdown of her marriage, as a friend when she faced divorce and royal exile.

As the pact said: 'You jump, I'll jump'. And when Fergie jumped in with both feet, the boss jumped in to rescue her.

KP was the first refuge Fergie sought when the divorce between herself and the Duke of York became absolute on 30 May 1996. I'll never forget the day when she came through the front door, stripped of her HRH status, devoid of her usual energy. As always, though, she displayed a strong front, laughing off that morning's newspaper headlines. 'We'll show 'em!' she told the princess, indicating a unity in the face of mutual marital strife because, in that same month, the boss's lawyers were thrashing out an agreement and divorce settlement for her too.

'We'll win in the end, won't we, Paul?' she said, looking across to me.

'Just keep smiling and hold your head high,' I said, and left them in private.

That summer, they went on holiday together to a mountain hideaway in the South of France with their children. The 'sisters' had never been closer.

It was on that holiday that a photo was taken of Eugenie, Beatrice, William and Harry together. It was an image to which both mothers referred as 'the future', and the princess used it in her last Christmas card. Whatever happened between her and Fergie, the princess adored Beatrice and Eugenie and kept that photo in a frame on her desk.

*   *   *

Other than being 'outsiders' experiencing marital breakdown, both ladies had something else in common: their strained relations with the matriarch of the House of Windsor, Queen Elizabeth, the Queen Mother—the true power behind the throne.

Wherever Her Majesty the Queen was at a residence other than Buckingham Palace, her mother was often invited as a house guest, which, in itself, caused a headache among the household over protocol. The Queen Mother was referred to as 'Queen Elizabeth' and Her Majesty as 'The Queen'. (In staff quarters, well away from royal ears, they were known less reverently as the 'Old Queen' and the 'Young Queen'.) The first indications I saw that the Queen Mother was 'anti-Diana' came one year at Sandringham where, during my time as footman to the Queen, she shared in the New Year festivities. She walked into the saloon drawing room as I was preparing the drinks tray and sat down near the magazine table, where the titles of *Tatler, Horse & Hound, Vogue* and *Harpers & Queen* were fanned out. The front cover of one bore an image of the Princess of Wales.

'She's *such* a silly girl!' the Queen Mother hissed, to her lady-in-waiting. Then, with a sleight of hand worthy of a magician, she flipped the magazine so that its front cover faced down. The princess was banished from view. In the last six years of the boss's life, the Queen Mother would not have a photograph or her name mentioned in her house. Correspondence from the Queen Mother, which had started with 'Darling Diana' and was signed 'Granny', dried up.

The princess once said that the Queen Mother had looked at her with pity in her eyes. What I witnessed that day told me that Queen Elizabeth couldn't bear the sight of her—and that moment stopped me in my tracks. Her action revealed her opinion of the boss, and her intolerance of the strife within the princess's marriage to her favourite grandson. By the mid-eighties, he had spent many hours confiding his side of the story to his grandmother, and she would only ever take his side, even though the boss's grandmother, Lady Fermoy, had been her close friend. As far as the Queen Mother was concerned, 'men had affairs, women did not'. In her eyes, the princess was to blame for not making her grandson happy.

In fact, the magazine might have featured an image of either the princess or the duchess, and the Queen Mother's reaction would have been the same. In her eyes, both ladies were 'trouble': one for causing misery to her grandson, the other for her 'unbecoming behaviour' as a member of the Royal Family. The Queen Mother had her own traditional views about how a lady should behave, and especially one with such a title. She, too, had also been a Duchess of York before her husband had succeeded to the throne as King George VI.

Ironically, both the princess and the duchess had slept at Clarence House, the Queen Mother's residence, on the night before their weddings. It was considered improper for them to leave Buckingham Palace—the groom's home—on the morning of their nuptials. 'She just left me to my own devices. I was another house-guest, not a bride-to-be,' the boss told me later. She had dinner alone, and there was no sense of occasion.

The princess and the duchess often compared notes on the Queen Mother, gossiping about her as if she were the grandmother-in-law from hell.

It has been suggested that they exacted a mischievous revenge for the Queen Mother's ice-cold treatment by ringing her late at night on her private line in her bedroom, then hanging-up. This is untrue as well as impossible: there was no direct line to her bedroom. All calls went via the switchboard and, unless it was the Queen or Prince Charles, the switchboard *never* put calls through to the Queen Mother so late.

What they *did* do was hijack the Queen Mother's Daimler one evening at Balmoral. The boss was Fergie's 'accomplice', she insisted, as she recounted that 'hilarious' episode. She drove and the duchess was a passenger as they tore round the castle's gravel driveways; roaring with laughter as they vented their frustrations by speeding along in the Queen Mother's vehicle. And they got away without being spotted.

Not that the boss and Fergie would have been laughing had 'darling Granny' ever caught on: everyone found her a formidable character whose quiet and gentle public persona was belied by the austerity she showed behind the scenes. She was a time-bomb packaged in a small, frail frame, with which no one dared tamper. She was a notoriously bad time-keeper, always running late, the only person who ever kept the Queen waiting.

If there was one thing that infuriated the Queen Mother, it was the knowledge that the boss was very much the 'People's Princess', whose global popularity threatened to undermine her grandson. She could ostracize the princess as much as she liked, but she could never defeat her. In that regard, I sensed that she knew she had met her match: the princess who shared the same steel will and determination to get her own way.

It always struck me how different the princess's relations were with Her Majesty the Queen. In the letter the princess wrote to me in October 1996, in which she predicted her death in a car accident, she also wrote: 'I just long to hug my mother-in-law and tell her how deeply I understand what goes on inside her.' It was the difference between a warm weather front, and a cold one.

The Queen Mother died peacefully in her sleep during the afternoon of 30 March 2002, at her country home, Royal Lodge, in the Great Park at

Windsor. She was 101, and had lived a wonderful, fulfilled life. I thought of Prince Charles that day, and how devastated he must be because, in my time at Highgrove, he had often said, 'I just don't know what I'll do when she's gone', and he meant it: tears welled in his eyes. The mere thought of her passing stirred him—she meant *that* much to him. He kept, on his desk, a miniature portrait of her as she was when she became consort in 1936.

*   *   *

Fergie and the boss shared a common fear: that 'spooks' within the intelligence services were monitoring them. The duchess asserted that she had learned MI5 were tapping their telephone lines. Another member of the Royal Family had also issued words of advice to the boss, 'You need to be discreet—even in your own home—because 'they' are listening all the time.'

The princess's worries about the security services will undoubtedly form part of the belated British inquest into her death. That process, as well as Scotland Yard's separate investigation into the conspiracy theories, will focus on the letter the princess wrote, and left for me, ten months before she was killed in the car crash in Paris. I published it in *A Royal Duty*, and those chilling, prescient words, written in October 1996, forced the authorities to arrange an inquest. It predicted: 'This particular phase in my life is the most dangerous. [A person's name] is planning 'an accident' in my car, brake failure and serious head injury in order to make the path clear for Charles to marry . . .'

203

The boss's mind-set at the time is bound to come under scrutiny, and I'm concerned that she may be painted as a neurotic paranoid, scared of her own shadow, and entertaining deranged thoughts. It wouldn't be the first time the system, and her enemies, have attempted to depict her as 'mad' and misrepresent her to the world. They did it when she was alive and they may use the opportunity to discredit her now that she's no longer with us.

So, it's important to understand *why* she was concerned for her safety in the final two years of her life. She was being *advised*. Not just by Fergie but by a former MI6 officer Fergie had introduced to her.

This individual became the 'security consultant' on whom the princess and the duchess relied. One weekend he visited KP to sweep the apartments for listening devices. None was found, but he advised the boss to remove a round convex mirror from above the fireplace in the sitting room because, with today's hi-tech surveillance techniques, 'listening wavelengths' can be transmitted into buildings and bounced back off mirrors. It was the certainty that she was being monitored that led the boss to worry about her safety. It preyed on her mind so much that she felt compelled to write down her fears, in the same way that she put pen to paper about countless other anxieties. For her, writing things down was cathartic. In all probability, the boss never expected that letter, entrusted to me for safe-keeping, to become significant. It was a 'just-in-case' form of insurance. The chilling truth is that its prediction of her death was all too accurate.

I don't know whether she ever told Fergie that she had written that letter, or whether the duchess was given a copy but they had many discussions about their security. Fergie was also advised about security and surveillance at Sunninghill Park. The two friends decided to use their adviser to 'hide' their mobile phone calls. Neither the boss nor Fergie used a landline for their most private conversations. They used their mobiles, and, to cover their tracks, they registered them in the name of the security consultant, the itemized bills went to his address. He would pay the amounts due, then invoice his royal clients, who sent him a cheque to cover the amount. It was a system designed to thwart the investigative British press, and the security services. The princess and the duchess were 'accomplices' once more.

*   *   *

If a thread of jealousy ran through the royal 'sisterhood', there was also an underlying sense of competition; a form of sibling rivalry writ large. From even the early days of their marriages, the boss thought Fergie was trying at times to outshine her—to portray herself as the even fresher 'breath of fresh air', or the daughter-in-law who could better impress the Queen. By Fergie's admission, in her book *My Story*, she said, 'The Queen probably thought, "Goodness, at last we have a sensible person around here . . ."' She added, 'From my initial success, I became a heroine, this simply wonderful person, the perfect addition to the Royal Family . . .'

The princess didn't resent this in Fergie, she

merely made a mental note of it. She had no time for resentment. It was, she said, a negative energy: 'Resentment is trying to change something that is just what it is. When we can't change it, we resent it.' The boss never once attempted to change Fergie. She was what she was. But it appeared that Fergie went out of her way to stand out, to be different, to be better, either deliberately or subconsciously. One stark example was her wearing of ladies' cotton gloves on public engagements.

The princess had long since decided to dispense with gloves, viewing them as a barrier when it came to shaking hands with the public. Whether she was warmly greeting an old lady in a crowd or shaking the hand of an AIDS patient, she was one for 'pressing the flesh', not pressing the flesh through a royal glove. The Duchess of York *always* wore gloves, just like the Queen.

And where the princess obsessed about 'doing the right thing' in the public's eyes, the duchess fretted about 'doing the right thing' in the eyes of the Royal Family. And probably still does.

If there was one area where she should have known better than to tread, it was the extra sensitive one concerning William and Harry. And no one, but no one, should have attempted to outdo the princess when it came to her sons. On one occasion, Fergie made that mistake. She was undoubtedly an adoring, lovable, considerate aunt but for someone who knew the boss so well, her generosity to William one Christmas was an error of judgment.

The princess had bought William a BB-gun from Forbidden Planet in Tottenham Court Road, in

London. I had been sent to the store to buy it, along with a bag of plastic pellets. But it was relegated to virtual abandonment because Fergie had gone one better, and bought him a night sight for his air rifle. William squealed with delight as if it was the best present in the world, and the aunt, not the mother, glowed. To know the love the boss had for her boys, and to know how fiercely she guarded being their No.1 woman, was to know that you *never* went one better with them.

The princess felt the present was 'too extravagant and too advanced' when, in truth, it was simply not the BB-gun. Not that she said anything to William. She certainly didn't want to be the one who spoilt his excitement after the duchess had given it to him. So, she masked her disapproval. William sat at his bedroom window at night, and targeted squirrels as they darted across the top of the walled garden.

'Whatever you do, don't shoot Princess Michael's cats, William!' she'd say. As far as he was concerned, the gift from Fergie had his mother's approval, and he didn't need to know otherwise. But the incident compounded tensions that, at KP at least, had been bubbling ever since Fergie had published her autobiography that same year.

My Story was Fergie's account of how her royal fairytale had unravelled so spectacularly, and she was proud of it. I remember the day when she breezed into KP, through the hallway and into my pantry, and left a mini-tower of copies on my desk. 'There you go, Paul,' she said. 'I thought you might like a few for your family and friends.' She had gone to the trouble of signing each one, 'Sarah 1996', on the red front inside page. She seemed oblivious to the tension her book had caused in the boss and she bounded up the stairs to see her. Privately, the boss was seething, because Fergie's story was littered with references to her. She was mentioned on nearly sixty-five pages. When the princess later spotted the copies in my pantry, she wanted to know what I was doing with so many. I explained that Fergie had dropped them off. The boss tutted. It was clear that she had already devoured the book, making more mental notes. 'What I don't understand,' she said, 'is why she had to talk about me more than herself!'

Of course, the princess was mainly upset that she hadn't been consulted about the extent of her inclusion in the book. She had not been given the chance to approve certain sections relating to herself, as she had done, for example, with Andrew Morton's *Diana: Her True Story.* Neither did she feel the book had been written with her interests in mind: some 'derogatory' comments had been made, she thought.

One offending section related to how the princess had loaned Fergie a pair of shoes, and the duchess had contracted verrucas. The press pounced on this story and turned a light-hearted quip into a two-page story with headlines which, in turn, dominated all the promotional television interviews for the book. The princess was livid and, she told Fergie, 'extremely distressed by your actions'. However much Fergie complained she had been 'taken out of context', the boss was pretty unforgiving. Or, as Fergie said, 'she never gave me an ounce of understanding'.

'I know I've pissed you off,' she pleaded, in a letter to the boss, 'but right now, I need a small centimetre of your friendship, understanding and support. I'm sorry.'

The princess would not budge even that far. As a result, Fergie blamed herself for, as she would later put it, 'sabotaging a beautiful friendship'.

Contrary to widespread belief, this was not the primary reason for the demise of their friendship but it was a contributory factor. In another passage, Fergie wrote about how much *she* missed Prince Charles being in *her* life—'I miss him more than he knows,' she wrote. '*She* misses him!' The princess tutted.

It was interesting that Fergie should have guessed how the boss would feel when she read certain passages about herself, because in *My Story* she recounted how she had felt when her father, Major Ronald Ferguson, had published his autobiography in 1994: 'That book left me feeling totally forlorn . . . It wasn't the content of what Dad had written. It was the fact that he had traded upon our relationship . . . without so much as consulting me.'

For a while, the princess bit her lip and said nothing as Fergie galloped through her book promotion, and every newspaper article focused on 'Fergie and Diana' or 'Life with Diana'. Increasingly, she grew more and more infuriated.

Eventually her patience snapped. 'I've had it with her—I've had it with this book!' she said.

Then Fergie went to America to promote it. I remember getting a phone call from my friend Chuck Webb who saw the resulting interviews, and how 'the Diana factor' had propped up the headlines and interviews. It had led to what the boss referred to as 'screaming headlines'. It was my unenviable duty, as her eyes and ears, to keep her informed of all that was unfolding on the other side of the Atlantic.

In a terse phone call in which the princess made her position clear, she asked Fergie to concentrate more on her own life, 'not my life', during TV interviews. 'This is *your* book!' she reminded her, 'Your moment, your story, not mine!'

My Story rocked the sisterhood that had, up until then, weathered so much. The princess saw the duchess lapping up the limelight at her expense. In turn, the duchess felt the princess was being over-sensitive and hypocritical, and a few choice words were exchanged in correspondence between them in November 1996. In the boss's mind, she had been 'hurt and wounded' and Fergie had crossed the boundaries of accepted behaviour within a friendship. The princess understood that the duchess needed to tell her story, but not if it included poking fun at her best friend, and left 'the entire country laughing at me'. After that, the tensions between them never really went away, and Fergie never visited KP again.

*   *   *

Events came to a head and this friendship ran aground in the summer of 1997 over something that, for the boss, was the final straw. The media had tried to suggest in the intervening years that the rift centred solely on the verruca story in the book. It did not: it may have been a contributory factor but it was not the only reason. I don't intend to divulge that reason, but the princess showed me the letter she had written to Sarah and she made her feelings abundantly clear. Throughout May and June, the princess refused to take her phone calls. The boss was for ever 'out' or 'unavailable'.

Fergie told me later that the letter was 'very distressing and heartbreaking' to read because the boss had been 'so judgemental, rash and final'. I knew that already because of the A4-sized envelope with the initial 'E', in a child's hand, in the bottom left-hand corner.

I sat in my pantry and took out a card from the envelope. Mounted on the front was a sepia photograph of a giggling Princess Eugenie, taken on a sunny day at Craigowan, a country house on the Balmoral estate.

Then the penny dropped. The 'E' on the envelope stood for 'Eugenie'. The young princess had written the envelope—giving the impression that the card was from niece to auntie. However, when I opened it, it was to see the very distinctive hand-writing of the duchess—making a final plea for their friendship to be repaired.

She must have known that had she written the envelope, it would have been sent back unopened, marked 'Return to Sender'. That was what the boss had done with unwanted letters from her mother and brother when their respective relationships broke down.

However, because Eugenie had written the envelope, and because it was her photograph on the front of the card, the boss had opened it and had seen what the duchess had written. Perhaps Fergie, having witnessed the princess's intransigence in the past, was not willing to take the risk and had asked her daughter to write the envelope. Maybe she needed to know that her old friend would at least read her words. And I'm convinced she also hoped that a picture of Eugenie would remind the princess of the good times they had shared as a family. Sadly, it only made matters worse.

I read Fergie's words with a sense of helplessness and my heart went out to her. She was clearly desperate to make amends, trying so hard to reach out to the boss. My dismay was compounded by the sure knowledge that the princess was in no mood for reconciliation. As all correspondence from the duchess, it started 'Dearest Duch'. But the first thing that struck me on immediately opening the card was not the message, which filled both sides of the card. It was the poem Fergie had taken the trouble to print out, mount on brown paper and glue to the centre of the card.

It was William Ernest Henley's 'Invictus' (meaning 'Unconquerable'), and the darkness of its words, the defiance of its tone and the personal struggle it depicted were almost autobiographical of the woman who had sent it. I wondered if it contained a hidden message.

Invictus
Out of the night that covers me,
Black as the pit from pole to pole,
I thank whatever gods may be
For my unconquerable soul.
In the fell clutch of circumstance
I have not winced nor cried aloud.
Under the bludgeonings of chance
My head is bloody, but unbowed.
Beyond this place wrath and tears
Looms but the Horror of the shade,

And yet the menace of the years
Finds, and shall find me, unafraid.
It matters not how strait the gate,
How charged with punishments the scroll,
I am the master of my fate:
I am the captain of my soul.

Fergie implored the princess to listen to her side of the story, not to be so judgmental and allow such negative energy to wedge itself between them. One phrase sticks in my mind because of the sense it spoke: 'After all we have been through together, I believe it's the very least we could give our souls . . .'

She couldn't have said it more clearly that her door remained open and whatever the princess chose to do, nothing would stop Fergie loving her and looking out for her. She mentioned that the boss was in her 'shell' again. I think she honestly felt, as I did, that in time the rift would be healed. It wasn't the first time in their friendship that there had been disagreement. And, as Fergie and I had learned from experience, 'no-speaking spells' had previously thawed. I had often talked to the duchess on the phone, listening, offering advice when I could, and her heart—if not her judgement—was always in the right place. At the end of 1994, she sent me a framed photo of her with Beatrice and Eugenie with a message that said: 'Dear Paul and Maria, thank you so much for your incredible kindness and support. Words are not enough but thank you. With best wishes— Sarah.'

She would discover, with some heartache, that words would not rebuild her relationship with the

213

princess. The boss had made it clear in her letter that she wanted no further contact with Fergie, and she had asked that neither of them discuss each other's lives with the media. 'Nothing will appear from this end!' the boss had written.

Fergie's response to that, I remember, was to scoff at that remark: she said if that was so, the princess would have to rein in her off-the-record briefings to Richard Kay, the *Daily Mail* journalist. The boss was infuriated by that because it echoed a phrase in a letter she had received from her brother in April 1996 when he wrote that he'd lost touch *'to the extent that I have to read Richard Kay to learn that you are coming to Althorp . . .'*

Although he was her friend, Richard Kay was an extra-sensitive issue with the boss because she laboured under the misapprehension that no one knew he was her discreet conduit. The truth was that her trust in him was one of the worst-kept secrets in Fleet Street.

In the days after she received that card from Fergie, she joined me on the staircase and we sat down to draft a response. Sadly, there was no softening in her stance and there was no getting through to her. She was intent on firing back an indignant reply. And she had a fresh bee in her bonnet—that Fergie had, as she saw it, the temerity to use Eugenie as leverage in a dispute between adults. 'When it comes to honesty, perhaps one shouldn't use one's child to address the envelope,' she scribbled. Then she said out loud, and wrote down, the one phrase that has stuck with me ever since. 'I'm happier than I've ever been.'

'Happier than I've ever been'—going into the

first week of July 1997, still with Hasnat, despite their ups and downs.

Happier than she had ever been—*before* Dodi Al Fayed.

I don't know whether or not the princess ever finished that letter, or whether she sent it. But Fate would ensure that a special friendship didn't find the peace it deserved.

Sarah, Duchess of York, did everything she could to make peace with the boss, and it was sad that events prevented their reconciliation. Later, I would witness a grief compounded with guilt when she turned to me after the boss's death, and asked me the one question for which I had no answer.

WISDOMS FROM KENSINGTON

She called them her 'wisdoms from Kensington', a vast collection of sayings, philosophies, spiritual insights and verses that provided a well of strength for a princess for ever searching to understand more about life, herself, her purpose and destiny.

She read William Wordsworth and William Butler Yeats for lessons about the soul and love. She delved into the wisdom of prophets such as Muhammad Iqbal and Kahlil Gibran, and she also relied on psychotherapy self-help books. It was from this reading that she drew her inner strength, beliefs and self-awareness, she said.

'If I don't understand who I am, how can I expect others to?' she'd say, when I caught her copying out a new pearl of wisdom, or when I found her in the sitting room, legs tucked beneath her, reading

215

what she referred to as her 'emotional Bible'—a book on personal and spiritual growth called *The Road Less Travelled*, by Dr Scott Peck. It's a self-help book about 'confronting and solving personal problems', and my wife Maria says millions of women have turned to it in their hour of need.

She *always* had that well-thumbed volume near to hand on her bedside table in case she needed to consult it for advice on emotional behaviour. More often than not, it was glued to her hands whenever she was going through a traumatic period in matters of the heart, or self-confidence or a setback in her well-documented fight against bulimia.

'I've had this book since 1988 and it's a constant guide,' she told me one evening. She had seemed engrossed in it and had failed to notice me standing in the doorway.

I didn't interrupt, cough or make a noise: it was correct to wait for her to address me. I just stood there, watching her read, with her hair pulled back with one of her cloth bands. When she looked up, a frown of concentration eased into an almost embarrassed smile. I must have come in at the right moment, though, because she asked if she could read something to me. I walked into the room a little further as she began. Then she stopped because I was still standing, and she beckoned me to join her on the sofa. Once more, duty was about to blur the line between professional butler and personal friend with an opinion to offer. When I sat down, she started the same section again. It had initally sounded like psycho-babble to me but I nodded in all the right places, and listened intently in an attempt at least to understand the subject matter.

Then she got to the point she had been so eager to share—it was something to do with the tools of self-discipline. '. . . and presidents and kings don't know how to use them!' she read out loud, and looked at me as if she had discovered a gem hidden among the pages. 'They don't—they don't!' she insisted. 'They don't know how to deal with life or its problems, and *that* is why they're all so emotionally and spiritually stunted.'

She seemed to be referring in general terms to the Royal Family but I interpreted this 'finding' as more of an observation about Prince Charles, whom she had always felt put his head in the sand when it came to confronting deeply personal and emotional matters.

'Perhaps you should buy him the book for his birthday, Your Royal Highness?' I suggested.

That idea got short shrift. 'It would be lost on him,' she said dismissively.

It was not unusual for her to share her discoveries and insights with other friends. She would repeat them over the phone or include them in correspondence, and always make a joke about why she felt a particular friend needed to know or share this 'life information'.

That was when she would jest about issuing 'wisdoms from Kensington' or end a letter with '. . . and here endeth the lesson from the Kensington area'.

It was after reading that section on 'the tools of emotional discipline' that the boss went to her desk, took a pen and a sheet of memorandum paper and started to make notes. She even entitled it 'Problems and Pain'. She wrote down a number of mental pick-me-ups, as if she was a student of psychology making bullet points from a piece of educational literature.

She copied out a quote from Benjamin Franklin: 'Those things that hurt, instruct.'

'Problems make us grow mentally and spiritually,' she wrote. 'What makes life difficult is that the process of confronting and solving problems is a difficult one.'

Then: 'Use our problems as opportunities to change our lives.'

This last phrase struck a chord in me on the journey to Angola when she had presented me with her thoughts on Calcutta. If you look back on what she said in 1992 after her visit to Mother Teresa's hospice, she ended her thoughts with almost identical words: '. . . having responsibility gives us the power to make changes in our lives . . . maybe it's time.'

People have often asked me, over the past decade, 'What was she like?' 'How did she think?' or 'What made her tick?' Some less generous individuals have even had the temerity to ask 'Do you think she was mad?'

The simple answer to all those questions is this: what made her so extraordinary was how ordinary she really was. She could have been so many women's ideal best friend. She harboured the same insecurities and self-doubts as you and I. In fact, I believe that the intense light of global fame and media scrutiny exacerbated her insecurities. The princess was a humble, genuine person, with a remarkable warmth and charisma, whose ordinariness, paradoxically, made her unique. There was nothing conventionally regal or stuffy

218

about her. She was that curious mix of strength and vulnerability. She loved life and embraced people. And the best and most natural thing about her? She was real. She was breathtakingly so, and it was the one quality that hit people between the eyes more than any other when they met her.

She wasn't at all mad but she was, as most humans tend to be, complicated and not without flaws. Yet she was always striving to be a better person and sought out myriad philosophies to 'train' herself to become mentally and spiritually stronger. She believed—or learned—that self-analysis was a healthy way of challenging herself. She said, 'It requires courage to turn yourself inside out.' Which was why she searched for answers and reasons from within her own problems and pain. Perhaps she gained strength from the maxim my mother passed down to me: 'everything happens for a reason'.

It wasn't only the wisdom of Dr Peck that influenced her. The princess had countless psychotherapy sessions with Susie Orbach, a therapist who specialized in eating disorders and played a vital role in helping the boss to understand and control her bulimia. Then there was Dr Mary Loveday, who addressed the chemical balance in the princess's body with her three-times-a-day vitamin prescriptions.

The princess was never embarrassed by her reliance on philosophies or therapists. She insisted that she *did* believe in them, and they *did* make sense of a lot of things. 'It helps me do the mental house-cleaning!' she joked.

All her philosophies and spiritual insights combined to strangle the insecurities and worries that seemed to haunt her, and once she had written them down or mentally rehearsed them, she drew strength from them. Sometimes she would stick Post-it notes on the windowpanes overlooking the walled garden or leave them propped up on her desk. In the end, there were dozens.

Her collection of philosophies helped her to cope with and understand why her marriage had failed, why her low self-esteem was rooted in her childhood. Indeed, they helped her to understand her own mind. She was a deep thinker, and we spent hours talking over and analysing her reactions to certain events. Other friends would share her introspective analysis, and she was capable of spending hours on the telephone. The boss was the first to admit that her low self-esteem and poor self-image ate away at her self-confidence and, in turn, at her marriage because they rendered her vulnerable and needy. She hung on to Prince Charles for the attention and recognition she craved, and when it was not forthcoming, the sense of rejection was crushing.

She wrote down her self-appraisal, taken from a philosophy, late one evening: 'Isolation in a relationship can cause us to derive too much of our self-esteem from one person, and it puts us in a position where if that person should reject us, the entire foundation of our self-esteem could be demolished.'

Way too late, she was examining her marriage, the needs she had had within it, the emotional burden she had placed on Prince Charles—a burden which had found him, as we all know, wanting because he, too, had emotional needs.

On the same memorandum sheet, she had added: 'Greatest barrier to bonding is low self-esteem itself—a woman with low self-esteem may choose to live without much intimacy.'

We sat on the stairs one evening and discussed the philosophies that became almost conclusions in her own mind; justifiable reasons as to why her marriage didn't—and couldn't—work. Commitment for her, she said, had led to pain in childhood and adulthood. She had learned at an early age that her parents had yearned for a son when she was born, and had never escaped the feeling that they would have preferred a boy. She was also deprived of a constant maternal bond because her mother, Frances Shand Kydd, had lost custody of her children in her divorce from Earl Spencer. She had felt abandoned by her mother, who had run off with Peter Shand Kydd. Then had come the harsh reality of boarding-school, and no sooner had she grown up than she was marrying into the harsh reality of the House of Windsor. It's easy to see how, in the mind of the princess, rejection was a constant thread in her life. To her, commitment meant pain. When she gave of herself, she only ever felt let down.

Which was probably why she reacted in such haste when she ended her relationship with Hasnat—because, she saw another rejection: someone else who wasn't up to the job of loving her and understanding her world. So she cut it off. Then threw herself into a reckless fling.

Any amount of self-help books would tell us that what she and Dodi Al Fayed shared wasn't real love. She had so much love to give others, yet when it came to receiving love, she felt let down by the people on whom she relied. I think she agreed with that summary when I floated it past her one evening as we sat on the stairs. Whenever I offered an opinion that was met with contemplative silence, I knew she was mulling it over.

Eventually, she replied: 'I've been a rather bad picker of men, and who would take me on anyway with all my emotional baggage?'

'He's out there. He's just waiting for you,' I reassured her more than once. Not that she believed me. At least, that was what her half-hearted smile told me. But she *was* getting stronger, and she *was* far happier than she had ever been—all because she'd started to understand herself better.

She had been able to bring a certain rationale to some irrational thinking. She had found extra confidence and, in the last year of her life, seemed less timid and less vulnerable—and, throughout it all, she never lost her sharp sense of humour, poking fun at her 'issues'. As she said, 'High self-esteem doesn't protect you, but it does allow you to entertain self-doubt without being devastated!'

I hope that by sharing some of her innermost thoughts, philosophies and beliefs with you, you will begin to understand the princess, and hopefully to concur with some of the adopted 'wisdoms of Kensington'. They were the pearls of wisdom she strung together to get herself through everyday life.

*   *   *

When my mum Beryl died in 1995, the princess gave me her copy of *A Road Less Travelled*. By that stage of her life, she was already seeking out different, often Muslim-influenced philosophies. I'll be honest: I didn't so much read the book as skim through it, but it remains a precious possession to this day because the princess's markings are scattered through it—as if her hand is still pinpointing the lessons in life she considered valuable.

As with every CD or book she owned, she identified it as her own by writing 'Diana' on the inside page. When I flick through it now, it reminds me of how much she relied on it. Sentences and phrases are underlined in blue and black pen, and her notes are in the margins of the pages. Some sections of text are blocked out with yellow highlighter pen, even if the colour has faded now. The odd corner has been folded back to mark a specific page. It is *The Road Less Travelled*—as travelled by Diana, Princess of Wales.

Self-image and self-worth were at the root of her self-doubt.

The princess had a huge hang-up about 'feeling valuable' to herself and others. She strongly believed that self-worth should be nurtured in childhood; and felt this had not happened for her.

'Feeling of being valuable is essential to mental health and the direct product of paternal love—such a conviction must be gained in childhood', she wrote down one day. From this, I know she began to realize that her 'problems' were not of her own making. 'Much of my self-image and many of the ideas I have about myself were acquired in childhood,' she admitted. 'It is the parents who undermine a child's self-esteem.' It was an astute observation rather than apportionment of blame.

This philosophy is significant, I think, in how she approached her role as mother to William and Harry, giving them constant love and attention and ensuring that the nanny's hand was *not* the one that rocked the cradle. She was determined that her children would feel valuable and cherished from the moment they were born, and she made sure of that. Mistakes that had been made in the rearing of the princess (through a sense of abandonment and lack of attention) and Prince Charles (through non-tactile almost cold paternal relations) would not be repeated by the Prince and Princess of Wales.

It is a tribute to her that William and Harry have grown into secure, confident, level-headed young men who both, outwardly at least, seem devoid of their mother's self-image issues and their father's fear of failure. I like to think that the boss nurtured her boys for long enough to instill in them the basic values and beliefs so dear to her. As the boss underlined in *The Road Less Travelled*: 'As a result of the experience of consistent parental love and caring throughout childhood, such fortunate children will enter adulthood not only with a deep internal sense of their own value but also with a deep internal sense of security.'

By far the most thumbed sections of the book focus on the distinction between neuroses and character disorders. The princess always felt she had a neurosis rather than a character disorder, which was why the theory peddled by some individuals—that she had some form of a borderline personality disorder—was poisonous nonsense. She felt that her 'neurosis' (which seems too strong a word to me) was her lack of self-worth and a chronic self-image problem, which had led to her bulimia. She blamed herself for her problems, yet strove to overcome them.

'Dissatisfaction with yourself is a habit pattern'—that appeared in blue ink on a memorandum sheet one day. Then: 'From a correct relationship to yourself comes a right relationship to all others and to the divine.'

Often, these philosophies were written down without a source; some came from Dr Scott Peck, others from elsewhere. I remember one day when we were in the dining room and she was having breakfast, reading the newspapers. For once, there was nothing about her. I made a joke about no news being good news and in response she delivered what was clearly a new pearl of wisdom: 'Be more concerned with your character than your reputation because your character is what you really are while your reputation is merely what others think you are!' In the privacy of KP, she had put the relevance of Fleet Street in its place.

Later that day, the same philosophy had been written on a memorandum sheet and propped on her desk. It was clearly the 'saying of the week'. When I queried where it had come from, she replied, 'I read it somewhere', and then she smiled.

Part of me felt she wanted me to think she had come up with it herself, and I found that endearing. The self-taught student of psychotherapy enjoyed sharing her 'wisdoms from Kensington' because she felt she was passing on something of importance to people whose welfare she cared about. Yet no one was learning faster than the woman herself.

*　　　*　　　*

The princess hated the idea of being perceived as a victim—'a victim' of the Royal Family, 'a victim' of her husband's betrayal, 'a victim' of the hand she had been dealt. 'I've seen real victims and real suffering and I am not a victim,' she said while her divorce was being finalized in the summer of 1996. Sure enough, she adopted a wisdom to support her point: 'If we play the victim role then we are using our personal power to be helpless. Responsibility gives us the power to make changes in our lives . . .'

'I'm not a victim because I'm taking charge of my own life,' she added.

The princess was as good as her word, and as good as the philosophy she wrote down: I never once saw her play the 'poor me' card in private. Self-pity was a curse she had been spared.

Of course, I and others witnessed her private distress, and we sat with her when she was in tears and wondering where she would find strength to cope with the next day. But she was never riven with bitterness. As the princess matured emotionally, and embarked on her spiritual and psychological journey, she offloaded the negative baggage that might have weighed her down during the 1980s. 'An unwillingness to forgive limits personal growth,' she wrote down one day and privately, as far as the happiness of Charles and Camilla was concerned, she even 'wished them well'. 'I have no hatred for him. Charles and I are friends and civil to one another,' she said, after her ex-husband had popped in one afternoon for a surprise cup of tea.

'Blame is about giving away one's power and

responsibility,' was another maxim she had copied down.

That was the amazing thing about the princess: she blamed no one for her childhood, her marriage or the isolation she felt within the Royal Family. But she acknowledged that a dysfunctional family background, coupled with the family into which she had married, was the cause of her heartache. She located the cause without seeking to blame, and cried buckets as she sought to put things right for herself.

Yet, one powerful emotion had to be channelled—anger. Many women found anger hard to express, she said, and read up on it. She needed to understand that anger and hatred were two different things. Soon she began to grasp that she wasn't alone in feeling anger over marital breakdown. Hundreds of thousands of ordinary women needed to scream when no one seemed to be listening. 'Believe that anger is natural,' she wrote. And 'Accept anger as a human emotion. Don't feel ashamed of it.'

Once she was comfortable with expressing anger, she hired a kick-boxer to come to KP with his 'punchbag' hands. Maybe it was all her trips to the gym at Chelsea Harbour Club but it sounded like she could pack a mean punch for someone who appeared so timid and kind. She never let me into the drawing room when the muscled expert arrived each week with his oblong, padded gloves. But the grunts, groans and aggression I heard coming from behind the door told me that the sessions were doing the trick. When the door opened, a red-faced, leotard-clad princess would emerge panting and smiling. 'I *enjoyed* that!' she would say.

I believe it was December 1992 that she began to view life differently, and seek the quiet counsel and wisdom philosophies. I think she went on a personal journey after an intense period of reflection between June, when Andrew Morton's book was first published, and Christmas, when the royal separation was announced. It had also been the year of her spiritual and humanitarian awakening in Calcutta. 'I was left stunned by the speed of events,' she admitted. 'Leading up to the publication of a book, life was unbearable. The bulimia kept knocking on my door, 'bringing up' the past fears . . . the unhappiness inside was torture day and night.' It was around that time that the boss said that everyone within the Royal Family seemed to have 'six pairs of eyes instead of one.'

That book was the final straw to the Royal Family but it provided the princess with a huge emotional release: she said it meant the pretence was over and people could know the truth.

She felt there were many turning points for her around that time. Although the press had been 'ghastly', she said the newspapers had realized that she was the 'genuine article doing a job for the love of people, *not* for my own glorification'. She also got her freedom. 'I was able to have a rest and re-evaluate my life,' she observed. It was then that she began to talk more about spiritual belief. 'And people listened!' she said excitedly, 'People actually listened!'

It was almost as if she couldn't accept that people were listening *to* her, couldn't grasp that they believed she had something of worth to say. Her need for approval was not satisfied by cheering crowds or public adoration: that, she feared, was down to her being the Princess of Wales, the public person, and not Diana, the private one. Once again, her opinion of herself had deafened her to the respect and love of the people who engaged with her simply because she was *not* the typical royal princess. They connected with her *because* she was Diana, the real person.

'I know, I know,' she'd say, when I told her this by way of reassurance. But I'm not convinced she ever did.

What she did feel, after publication of the Andrew Morton book and the airing of her marital misery, was that the British public—especially the women—could relate to her better. 'I think they had a choice at that point, to back me or go against me—and they backed me,' she once said.

When she realized she *was* being listened to and that her input *did* make a difference, her self-confidence increased and spurred her on to working with the sick, the dying, the poor and the suffering. The work made her feel, as she put it, 'replenished'.

It was as if all the tears and suffering had led the princess to that crucial point in her life. 'My bulimia stopped. People followed me, not the other way round. Fears went. I was able to smile from within and on the outside. I was also recognized as having a brain—a good one at that.'

By the end of 1992, she had reached a point in her life that she had not thought possible half-way through that year. For the next five years I believe she grew stronger and stronger, happier and happier. Emotionally, it was her coming-of-age.

There were funny moments amid all the self-analysis. I still laugh when I remember the smell of incense from the joss-sticks she burned in her bedroom. The scent wafted through KP and I half expected to find hippies getting mellow in the sitting room! Neither I nor the housemaids ever quite understood the 'good' of joss-sticks. 'They stink the place out!' moaned Lily, the Filipina maid, and as soon as the princess had left for the day, she'd go round spraying air-freshener.

And of course there were the crystals, which featured in a big way at KP. The boss believed in their healing powers, and felt they brought a positive energy into her home; she had read about their calming and protective properties, and I was despatched regularly to Gregory, Bottley and Lloyd—a crystal warehouse in Chelsea just behind Stamford Bridge football stadium. There—with the boss's shopping list—I purchased rose and clear quartz, amethyst and amber to add to her personal collection or give away as gifts. Prince William's eighteen-inch stalagmite with its front section removed to expose a purple and violet crystal interior shell for his mummy's birthday took pride of place at one side of the fireplace in the sitting room. She also kept a giant rose quartz on her bedside table beside a photograph of William and Harry in their Ludgrove school uniforms, and a Russian icon of the Madonna and child.

Crystals, joss-sticks, astrologers, healers, psychics, philosophies and readings—the boss relied on them all. As I've said, if it helped, it was good.

Only now do I wish that I had sat down with her properly and discussed her conclusions about herself, and asked the question to which I need to know the answer—did you ultimately find inner peace and understand all that you hadn't understood about yourself? In *A Road Less Travelled,* she highlighted this sentence: 'Only a relative and fortunate few continue until the moment of death exploring the mystery of reality, ever enlarging and refining and redefining their understanding of the world and what is true . . .'

She was always reviewing and reworking her idea of her world and where she was headed. She had a lovely way of putting it: 'Life is like a constant tape—sometimes not the reality of your being, and it can be erased or re-recorded.'

I'd like to think she *had* 'found' herself, guided by the inner voice she said steered her. Certainly, much emotional fog had dispersed and she had a greater understanding of who she was. She was stronger than ever mentally, and had found her purpose in life, with the humanitarian path she was following.

And to return to the question of what she was like, I think part of the answer lies in a verse she wrote out for herself and to give to friends. My copy was left for me in my pantry. It was written in 1906 by Howard Arnold Walter, entitled 'I Would Be True'. If ever the voice of the princess could be heard today, I'd like to hear it reading this:

I would be true for there are those who trust me
I would be pure for there are those who care
I would be strong for there is much to suffer
I would be brave for there is much to dare
I would be friend of all, the foe and the friendless,
I would be giving—and forget the gift
I would be humble, for I know my weakness
I would look up, and laugh and love and live!

*   *   *

The princess was a deeply spiritual person. By this, I don't mean she believed in the afterlife or, as her psychic Rita Rogers may have put it, 'the other side'. It went much deeper than that.

She believed there was a realm beyond the physical presence; answers and meanings that came together to create an individual's pre-planned destiny. It wasn't a belief that stemmed from Christianity: she believed in God and embraced all faiths, from the Church of England to Roman Catholicism, Islam to Hinduism. It was a belief that grew from her own life experience and reading, and she believed that the journey of the soul was far more fundamental than the journey of the body—the shell, as she saw it, of the soul. She believed in the development of a higher state of consciousness. Indeed, she felt that the collapse of the Berlin Wall, and an ever-expanding freedom within Europe, was one example of an expanding consciousness among people. In that regard, she was someone who 'thought outside the box'. Ultimately, her philosophies combined to bring about one thing: the growth of the human spirit.

Some of those who work in the media, and others naturally inclined against her, may dismiss this aspect to her character as eccentric, especially in Britain—for me, this country lost its faith and spiritual guidance long ago. It's now a place where anything more than the odd prayer is dismissed cynically as 'God squad' or 'wacko'. But as the princess would have said, 'Judgments are limitations.'

Whether her deep sense of spirituality makes you laugh or frown or even sparks interest, *this* was what the princess was all about; *this* was how she thought, and those were the deep-rooted beliefs that guided her in everything she did. She was always looking for ways to expand and enlighten herself.

One poem she wrote out in full is perhaps the best illustration of her spiritual vision and her sense that her childhood experience influenced the adult she became. She found inspiration in William Wordsworth's 'Ode: Intimations of Immortality From Recollections of Early Childhood'. In her own hand, she wrote out excerpts from the poem:

> *Our birth is but a sleep and a forgetting;*
> *The Soul that rises with us, our life's Star,*
> *Hath had elsewhere its setting,*
> *And cometh from afar;*
> *Not in entire forgetfulness,*
> *And not in utter nakedness,*
> *But trailing clouds of glory do we come*
> *From God, who is our home . . .*

She copied out that poem on Balmoral Castle-headed stationery, which she kept for inspiration at KP.

It was the death of her friend Adrian Ward-Jackson in August 1991 that brought the princess's interest in spirituality to the fore. His passing, as the princess and Angela Serota stayed with him in his hospital room, had a profound effect on her and she became fascinated with the 'journey of the soul', and the idea that death was a new beginning.

233

It was after Adrian had died that she bought *Facing Death and Finding Hope*. It was billed as 'a guide to the emotional and spiritual care of the dying'.

When Mum died, the princess instilled in me that: 'When a person dies, their spirit hangs around to watch for a while'. She believed that when a spirit is happy and content, it moves on to the next plane, which she felt had a window on this one. She also reminded me of some words of William Wordsworth: 'We will grieve not, rather find strength in what remains behind . . .'

Without the princess and the comfort she provided, I don't know how my dad or I would have got through those days after we lost Mum.

We talked about death and grief often at KP. I told the princess that had I not worked for the Royal Household, I'd probably have become a priest. She laughed hysterically at the idea, as had my classmates in the mining village of Grassmoor when I wrote an essay about that at school. I learned a lot from the princess in those dark conversations. She expanded my thinking and, ironically, I drew strength from her advice when she died two years after Mum. I honestly don't know how I kept standing, let alone functioning, in the days after she was killed but I like to think that her spirituality propped me up.

Soon after Mum's death, we had spent a grim evening discussing death and grief in our usual spot on the stairs when she told me how she had coped after her beloved father had died. The conviction that he was still a presence watching over her was the one thing that had kept her going, she said. She didn't fear death: she feared insanity more than death. Her words, not mine. She told me never to underestimate the capacity of the dying to give—in the same way Adrian Ward-Jackson's death had enlightened her, and the love she had felt in the room when he passed away.

That night she threw me three more 'wisdoms from Kensington', and I've never forgotten them. 'Some people fail to reach the psychological and spiritual destination of acceptance before death occurs.'

'Bereavement is an experience of change and adjustment.'

She told me to grieve openly for Mum. 'The tears move through us, wash us clean and create the space for something new.'

I also remember that she quoted from memory—and perhaps inexactly—*The Little Prince* by Antoine de Saint-Exupéry. She quoted it and later wrote it down: *'And at night you will look up at the stars . . . and in one of the stars I shall be living. I have to go to the stars. And one day, when you look at the stars, you will remember me.'*

I wasn't the only person to whom she quoted that. Now it seems powerfully prophetic.

The reassuring smile she gave me as she read out those philosophies lifted me, as did her sheer belief in what she was saying.

'When a person dies, their spirit hangs around to watch for a while.'

She believed it, so I believed it.

'Remember, Paul, she's still with you, and will always be with you,' said the boss, then got to her feet, wished me goodnight, and went to bed.

In August 1997, I needed to believe that more than ever.

IN MEMORIAM

The princess was lying on a bed with a white sheet across her body when I first saw her in the hospital. All I could see was her serene face 'asleep', and her red-painted toenails. Nurse Beatrice Humbert was standing to my left, and the boss's driver, Colin Tebbutt, to my right, pillars of support.

What I witnessed in that room was beyond distressing but I carried out my duties, ensuring that the boss was dressed in a black cocktail dress and a pair of matching shoes; that the morticians used her favourite lipstick and powder; that Mother Teresa's rosary—the one from her writing desk—was placed in her hand. Everything had to be done properly, as she would have expected, before we could bring her home to England.

But before we left that room in Paris's Pitie-Salpetrière Hospital, Nurse Humbert—whose support had been immense throughout the day—turned to me and said, in broken English, 'I think you should take this.'

Either she or Colin—and in the daze of that day I still don't remember which it was—took my hand, pressed something into my palm and closed my fingers round it.

I opened my hand and there was the gold band the princess had told me about just two days earlier; a Bvlgari, ridged dress ring patterned with sections of tiny pavè diamonds in the shape of an hour-glass. It wasn't particularly striking—it was very plain, very simple. It didn't strike me as custom-made because it was an 'open' band, designed to adjust to fit any finger. So it was a standard dress ring, not even measured for the boss's finger—emphasizing, again, its lack of significance.

In that instant, I remembered her giddiness as she told me about that ring, and my eyes stung with tears. It was another unbearable memory, handed to me as she lay just a matter of feet away. I looked at the ring. I looked at her 'sleeping'. I remembered her laughter from just 48 hours earlier. I was too choked to say a word to Nurse Humbert or Colin. It had been an emotionally horrendous day, and now the last of her possessions had been handed over. I had already been presented with a rectangular brown envelope that contained the rest of her jewellery, including the bracelet, which had lost half of its seed pearls during the crash, and one earring from the pair Dodi had given to her. The other was somewhere in the wreckage and, to the best of my knowledge, has never been found. I stood there, staring at the ring, for what seemed an age, rolling it between thumb and finger. It was a classical Bvlgari design which I later learned belonged to the 'Parentesi Collection'. It could never have been presented as an engagement ring. It could not even have passed for an eternity ring as they have diamonds all the way round the band. The ring in my hand was a dress ring in yellow gold—one of Bvlgari's most famous creations—and it could not have been more different to the so-called 'engagement ring'. That ring—which has always been described as a star of diamonds with a rectangular emerald at its centre—was, we've been led to believe, ready for collection by Dodi on August 30, providing a reason for the last-minute trip to Paris. But he had, by then, already presented a much simpler band to the boss—no star of diamonds, no rectangular emerald, no complete band.

Fourth finger, right hand. The phrase kept going over and over in my mind. That was the finger from which the doctors must have removed the ring. I know she was wearing it when she died because there was dry blood among the tiny diamonds.

Eventually I dropped it into the envelope, which I folded in half, and put into my trouser pocket for the flight home, with the princess's coffin, aboard the Queens Flight BAe 146 to RAF Northolt, London.

During the following traumatic week at KP, the luggage arrived from Paris. I was with the boss's sister, Lady Sarah McCorquodale, and her mother, Mrs Frances Shand Kydd, in the dresser's workroom to open two black leather suitcases complete with the gold 'D' monogram. Dresser Angela Benjamin steeled herself to unpack, launder, fold and put away the princess's clothes, even though she would never return. All three women unpacked the cases, and it was then that I noticed the empty Bvlgari presentation boxes.

I would expect Dodi's father to have known about these purchases. What Mr Al Fayed cannot do now is dispute that she was wearing his son's ring—one that she had only accepted in friendship. It is inconceivable that this was a precursor to an engagement ring. No man would present a ring of this type if an engagement was imminent.

Later, standing in my pantry, I showed Lady Sarah and Mrs Shand Kydd the Bvlgari jewels. I

238

didn't explain to the boss's sister and mother the story behind the dress ring, or the excitement—and relief—that had surrounded the surprise gift, the princess would have expected me not to. I do remember Mrs Shand Kydd's reaction when she saw the jewels: she virtually dismissed them, as if she suspected that her daughter had received the jewels from Dodi or, at least, had bought them in his company. She gave her frank and outspoken opinion—as I had heard before, as the princess had heard before—of the type of men her daughter had been dating. It was a personal and insulting tirade against Muslim men and, more specifically, Dodi Al Fayed and his father. Both are decent gentlemen who shared the fondness of the princess. At the time, I had neither the inclination or the energy to speak against such nonsense. But she almost recoiled from those jewels because of the link they demonstrated. They were ultimately returned to Althorp with boxes of the boss's belongings. It is right that the truth about the ring is now told because it was, unmistakably, given in friendship only.

And the consequence of that inescapable fact is that it removes the motive behind one of his conspiracy theories: that the princess was due to marry a Muslim, which was why she was killed. Neither the security services nor anyone else had an imminent marriage to prevent. If the services had been monitoring that relationship, and the private phonecalls, they would have known all about that 'friendship' ring, and that there was no prospect of an engagement. So that particular conspiracy theory can no longer be relevant. That is not to say that there is nothing to investigate, and many questions to answer, over the car crash in Paris. But the world must stop believing that Diana and Dodi were due to get married, because that is not the truth.

* * *

The princess never liked the dark—she slept with her bedroom door ajar to let in a dim shaft of illumination from the dressing room. Before I left KP at the end of every day, it became a habit to switch out every light except that one when the boss had gone to bed. Even when we travelled abroad, a light had to be on outside her door. She slept better, she said, with the comfort of light around her.

I remembered that when it came to the night of Friday 5 September 1997, when she and I were left alone for one last time, after she had been brought home on the eve of her funeral.

'Let me look after her one final night, and let her leave from her front door one last time,' I had pleaded with the Spencer family and royal advisers. They agreed, as did the Queen. KP had been her home for more than eighteen years. So she spent her final night not in the cold greyness of the Chapel Royal, where her coffin had lain that previous week, but in the warmth of her home, in the yellow-painted vestibule, between the front entrance hall and the door to the main staircase. That was where I held an all-night vigil beside her coffin, which rested on a trestle and was draped in the red, gold and blue of the Royal Standard.

It was ten o'clock at night by the time all her visitors had come and gone, having said a final

240

farewell. I closed and bolted the front door. Only the Right Reverend Richard Charteris, Bishop of London, remained in Apartments 8 and 9, sitting in silent prayer on a chair round the corner in the hall.

I kept vigil—doing my duty—beside the princess. When I had seen her on a hospital bed in Paris, she had looked fast asleep. That was what I had told myself at least: 'She's asleep. She's asleep.'

Wake up. Please wake up.

Her voice, in my mind, kept me standing. 'When a person dies, their spirit hangs around to watch for a while.'

I struggled to accept her death, just as I couldn't accept mum's passing, because I needed to believe she was still with us.

At KP, it comforted me to believe she was only asleep. And I knew that when she was sleeping, what comforted *her* was light.

So, I turned off all the lights inside the palace, every single one. And lit fifty candles.

Earlier I had placed them around that room, interspersed among the bouquets of white lilies, white tulips and white roses sent by friends and brought in off the street.

As I lit each candle, it sent flickering shadows dancing on the yellow walls, and the lobby became increasingly warm. I sat on a chair with my left hand on the coffin, the right hand holding pages of prayers and a Biblical text. I started to talk to her and continued all night. I told her what her mother and I had done for her in the Chapel Royal before the coffin had been bolted shut.

*   *   *

The whole world seemed to telephone KP in the week after her death. Many callers had the direct line, the number I answered, which has since been disconnected. In the most distressing week of my life, I was a reluctant switchboard operator. As soon as I put down the receiver, the phone would ring again. Her inner circle, her celebrity friends, her alternative therapists, the fitness instructors, the hairdressers, the fashion designers and members of the Royal Family all rang, turning to me with their grief, asking their own searching questions, offloading their feelings. Some with unhealed rifts—like her mother and Sarah, Duchess of York—wanted to know if she had spoken about them, if they had been privately forgiven. I felt like a priest, listening to everyone's grief but my own. Eventually, the phone was taken from me, presumably for my own good.

But the one call I had received, and wanted to take, was from the one person I knew would be hurting the most—Hasnat. When he rang and said he needed to see me, there was no doubt that we would meet.

There was nothing I could say or do to ease his grief, nor he mine. But this man had been, it seemed, an indispensable part of everyday life at KP until July that year, and it seemed right for us to meet. We agreed on the evening of Thursday, 4 September, two days before the funeral, which he would also attend at Westminster Abbey.

I hadn't wandered far from KP until that evening, or watched much television because I had been consumed with grief, the phone calls, the protection of that secret world, the preparations

242

for the all-night vigil, the funeral and the burial ceremony at Althorp. I had seen and felt only the grief inside KP.

But when I stepped outside for my clandestine meeting with Hasnat, the people's grief hit me equally hard. Traffic was almost at a standstill in Kensington High Street, and thousands of people were carrying bouquets, candles and photos of the princess, all streaming towards those black and gold gates. I could not believe my eyes. It was intensely moving to see such widespread and profound grief.

Look how much you are loved. Just look at how popular you are.

She would never have believed it.

I had operated on auto-pilot that week, unable to feel anything but pain and loss. Until I stepped outside, I'd thought real grief had been restricted to those who really knew her, but I couldn't have been more wrong. I had no idea that complete strangers on the streets could feel the same pain and loss, albeit in a different way.

I had gone out to meet Hasnat because he could never have come to KP as he once did.

He had been a secret visitor and his presence would have aroused suspicion, so we had agreed to meet at the bottom of the drive, adjacent to the Royal Garden Hotel.

Just before I left Apartments 8 and 9, I had been at my desk when I noticed the dark blue cloth band that the princess had used to tie back her hair. She must have taken it off while we were chatting in the pantry one day and forgotten it.

Instinctively I picked it up and brought it to my nose. It smelled of the Hermès perfume, Faubourg

24, she used. Her unmistakable scent. And that elasticated cloth band was one accessory I'll always remember, on her head, scraping back her hair, on the sun-lounger in the garden, on the sofa in the sitting room or at the breakfast table in the dining room. It was a unique scent and an unimportant yet precious personal possession. I slipped it into my pocket and headed for my rendezvous.

I waited anonymously on the pavement outside the hotel for almost an hour before I saw an arm waving to me from a battered old car, stuck in the crawling early-evening traffic. When Hasnat pulled up alongside me, he wound down the side passenger window. He looked awful, as if he hadn't slept for days; his eyes were dark and baggy, and his hair was unkempt. He looked as if he had just crawled out of bed.

'I had to see you,' he said, leaning across the seat to shake my hand through the window. 'Thank you for meeting me.' He squeezed my hand and we stared at each other, not knowing what to say. I didn't get into the car, just leaned through the window.

He had asked to see me but, once there, we hardly spoke. We didn't need to; it was almost as if seeing each other was enough. I think he just wanted contact with the world he had once known, with someone who had been aware of how close he once was to the boss, and how much he had meant to her. All week, he had been alone with his grief, unable to talk to anyone about it. It was ironic that he had been reduced, in his own mind, to just another mourner in the public throng outside KP, just a face in the crowd, yet his secret grief was greater than that of all those outside the gates.

When he let go of my hand, he fought back tears and nodded, ready to disappear back to his flat.

'Wait,' I said, 'I have something for you.'

I reached into my pocket, brought out the worthless piece of dark blue cloth and pressed it into his hand. His eyes brimmed with tears. Now he had something of the princess's; it would mean more to him than it would to anyone else. He held that hair tie to his nose and mouth for a second or two, breathing in her scent, and then put it into his pocket. He nodded, tried to say something, but couldn't. 'I'll see you at the funeral,' I said. 'Keep strong.' And he was gone.

I've since thought how pathetic that meeting was—we should have said so much more to each other but the loss of the princess had rendered us mute. Yet we had found comfort in our meeting. I walked back to the palace knowing the princess would have approved.

*   *   *

In the days before my all-night vigil, while the coffin was in the Chapel Royal at St James's Palace, on a low bier in front of the altar. I joined the princess's mother, Mrs Frances Shand Kydd, and her two sisters, Sarah and Jane, inside the chapel and we walked down the nave towards the princess in her English oak, lead-lined coffin. In the absence of her brother, I was there supposedly to provide strength for the women around me, yet I could not have felt weaker. It seemed cold, damp and dim.

Earlier that week, I had visited the chapel with Lucia Flecha de Lima. Not one candle had been

245

lit, and there was not a flower to be seen. Outside, there were millions, but inside nothing. A furious Lucia soon put that right, ensuring that the Right Reverend Willie Booth, the Queen's chaplain, brought flowers from the street into the chapel. The Brazilian ambassador's wife knew how to make things happen. She also arranged for bouquets to be delivered by the boss's florist, John Carter.

There was another noticeable change when I arrived at the chapel with the Spencers. As we approached the coffin, we saw that the lid had been pushed marginally to one side, revealing a one-foot gap at its narrowest end. I had endured the trauma of seeing her body on that hospital bed in Paris and wasn't sure I could bear to see her again. Not like that. I had known that the lid would be removed at some point. I just hadn't expected to walk in and find it already pushed to one side. Nothing, even when you're expecting it, can prepare you for a shock like that. I took a deep breath and tried to be strong as my eyes almost refused to look down. Thankfully, all I saw was the white lace of the interior but it still chilled me to know that she was in there.

Mrs Shand Kydd interrupted the awkward silence: 'I thought it better this way,' intimating that it was more seemly than having the lid removed completely.

The Royal Standard that would drape the coffin on its journey to KP hadn't arrived so I could see the brass nameplate, which read: 'Diana, Princess of Wales 1961–1997'.

We stood there for a few moments in the silence, knowing we had to perform the sombre task we had gone there to do, at my request, and with the agreement of the family. It was what the boss had done at her father's funeral, and I had done at my mother's. Also, it was because the boss *needed* to be surrounded by the love of her boys. As I said earlier, I knew what would comfort her in death as in life. In Paris, they had put rosary beads in her hand before she was placed in the coffin. It was now time to put beside her some personal, treasured items.

I had walked into the chapel with a small bag containing possessions I knew the boss would want to take with her on her final journey. I handed them one by one to Mrs Shand Kydd who was standing in front of me, nearest to the coffin. I had selected each item, without interference from anyone else, earlier that day at KP.

There was the teddy bear she'd had since she was a girl; her mother put it beside her daughter's feet.

There was a treasured photograph of her father wearing his flat cap on a shooting party, and I handed it to Mrs Shand Kydd almost apologetically—but this wasn't the time to worry about the minefield of family politics: all that mattered was what had been important to the princess. I suspect Mrs Shand Kydd appreciated that, too, because she didn't hesitate to place the photograph carefully—even though there was no accompanying image of herself. Then I reached inside the bag for the most important items: a photograph of William and another of Harry.

Earlier, I had gone into the boss's dressing room, sat down on the bamboo chair in front of the oval mirror and looked down at the pictures of her boys, beneath the glass top on her dressing-table.

She had surrounded herself with pictures of them because she loved them more than life itself. I smiled as Mrs Shand Kydd placed them inside the coffin, and both Jane and Sarah felt the weight of that gesture, too, because they started to weep quietly. Then we knelt in the front pews for ten minutes. I didn't say a prayer. Instead I remembered the night at KP when we had discussed death, spirituality and the journey of the soul. I remembered her quoting from *The Little Prince*, and a line by William Wordsworth: 'We will grieve not, rather find strength in what remains behind . . .'

Her voice repeating her 'wisdoms from Kensington'.

'When a person dies, their spirit hangs around to watch for a while.'

'The tears move through us, wash us clean and create the space for something new.'

'Remember, Paul, she's still with you, and will always be with you.'

Mrs Shand Kydd gripped her rosary as she knelt beside me, distraught. During the island burial at Althorp, she would say: 'At least I had her for nine months, Paul. All on my own.'

In those days when relations were trusting between the Spencers and me, I gripped her hand and said: 'She'll *always* be with you, Mrs Shand Kydd.'

*   *   *

When I first came back from Paris, there was only one place for me to find comfort, and that was at work. It was so difficult to be inside Apartments 8

248

and 9 without her there, knowing she would never come back. Yet, those walls contained memories that were comforting, even though I couldn't stop myself crying. I wandered in and out of the rooms, lost in a place I knew like the back of my hand. I sat at the dining-table and recalled our conversations. I sat on the sofa in the sitting room and imagined her sat beside me. I sat at her desk and thought of her writing. I sat at her piano and remembered her playing.

I went into her wardrobe room to pick up the scent from her clothes. And then I went into her bedroom and sat on the edge of her bed, the cream duvet with its orange tulip print. On each bedside table, there were crystals and photographs of her boys. I was in the boss's most personal space, and I must have sat there for hours on most days that week, sitting in silence, staring into space. My only company was the princess's collection of teddy bears and other cuddly toys that filled an entire sofa pushed against one of the bedroom walls. There was even the 'Gingham Frog' with the name-tape 'Diana Spencer' sewn under its eyes, dating back to 1975. It was her favourite in a collection she had amassed since boarding-school. There were teddy bears in pink-striped, bespoke Turnbull & Asser pyjamas. She even ensured her teddies dressed well! Another bear was made entirely out of chocolate brown mink, and one was falling apart, with one eye and one arm. And there were other bears, given to her by her boys, by her friends, by the men she had known; each one a memory, and never far away. I, among few others, knew how special those bears were to her, and the stories they could have told.

Shared knowledge was a source of mutual strength for many of her friends at that time. I drew strength from the inner circle, one of whom was Susie Kassem, an interior designer who presided as a magistrate in London. She had known the boss since 1995 and they would speak on the phone up to four times a day. On some Saturdays, the boss was invited round to her home in Chelsea for lunch. She also spent Boxing Day with Susie and her husband Tarik in 1996—her last Christmas.

I'll never forget Susie's first impression of life at KP. She was a little overawed when she first stepped through the front door but then she realized it was a far from ordinary royal household; it was a happy ship, relaxed and informal. She compared it to 'visiting a family of friends'. Susie was in New York when news filtered through to her that the princess had been involved in a fatal car accident with Dodi in a Paris underpass. She boarded the first plane to London. She bought some flowers, laid them at the front gate of the palace, like everyone else, then went to church. The next day she visited me at Apartments 8 and 9, and we cried together. Susie, like the princess, is a very spiritual lady and instinct told her that she needed to pay her respects inside her dear friend's home.

For Susie, the focal point for her grief was the full-length Nelson Shanks portrait hanging on the main staircase, above the grandfather clock. We remembered how the boss had thought she looked as if she was 'about to jump off a bridge' and laughed at the memory.

Then we each lit a tea-light and placed it on the

carpet, at the foot of the portrait, and said a few prayers with our heads bowed, holding hands. I offered Susie the opportunity to pay her private respects to the boss in the Chapel Royal, but she declined politely because, she said, 'It would be wrong of me to be afforded such a privilege when so many other people outside would want to be there as well.' So she joined the mammoth public line that snaked down the Mall and queued overnight to sign the book of condolence.

Raine Spencer also visited that week, and insisted on sitting in the drawing room. 'I feel closest to her in here,' she said, then she told me of 'what a good friend' the princess had been to her.

'It was such a pleasure to see her so in love with Dodi,' she remarked. I said nothing. So she pressed on. Then she mentioned something about marriage. And I said nothing, just listened. 'Do you think they *really* were in love?' she asked, the question no doubt raised by my silence.

Immediately, I thought of Hasnat and the meeting we'd had, how far away from the picture he was, and how wrong that seemed. I looked at Raine Spencer, nursing a cup of tea and *wanting* to believe—like the rest of the outside world—that Dodi had been her true love. At that moment, I didn't have the heart to tell her otherwise. It wasn't the time or the place for such a complicated conversation, especially with a dear friend of Mohammed Al Fayed. I opted for the diplomatic answer: 'She was having fun and she was happy.'

Many good people visited KP that week: Lisa Yacoub, daughter of Sir Magdi Yacoub, the eminent heart surgeon, came armed with a new collection of crystals and some poetry to comfort

251

me. There was the famous friend who gave me the thirty-second answering-machine message—'something small' to make me remember and smile. There were also heartfelt letters from Princess Michael, and the Duchess of Kent. William and Harry came home that week, too, accompanied by Prince Charles. I was waiting for them in the inner hallway. I'll never forget how Harry burst through the front door and hugged me. Then came William, reaching out to shake my hand, like his father. Their courage was astounding as they sorted through their possessions in the nursery. I cried so hard when they left that afternoon—KP had never seemed so sad and empty when they were there.

Sarah, Duchess of York, rang constantly until the phone was taken away from me. Banished from the inner circle and unable, despite her best efforts, to heal her rift with the boss, she was tormented with her grief. It seemed I was the only person to whom she could turn for answers, but I was unable to provide the absolution I felt she was looking for.

'Do you think she would have forgiven me?' she asked, in one of many conversations. Just as I had with Raine Spencer, I opted for a diplomatic answer: 'Wherever the princess is now, Your Royal Highness, all is known and you have your memories,' I told her. After that, she didn't ask any more questions.

One special visitor to KP that week was Rosa Monckton whose grief was compounded by the knowledge that she would be unable to visit Apartments 8 and 9 and, more especially, the walled garden where her daughter Natalia had been secretly buried for three years. She still had the key that the princess had given her. But in the week of the funeral, she knew she had to relinquish it. She handed it back but not before she had made a final request—that a photograph be taken of that corner beneath the tree. So we took that photograph as a permanent reminder of that special place, a special day and the princess's unforgettable act of kindness.

*   *   *

Visitors kept coming and going but, all the time, I had been meticulously planning my vigil and farewell on the eve of the funeral.

Father Tony Parsons—the priest I'd sounded out about a secret wedding ceremony for the boss and her 'Mr Right'—was the last person to visit before the coffin arrived. He brought with him two huge ivory church candles, which I placed on silver stands, to add to the fifty I had placed around the vestibule, and then he splashed the room with holy water. He handed me copies of prayers to read, and gave me a text from the Gospel according to St John. The two of us said a prayer, and then he left. I was in my black suit and tie, ready for when the coffin arrived.

Moments later, I heard the hearse pull up outside, footsteps on the gravel, then the double front doors opening. The coffin was carried down the hallway and into the vestibule; the woman who had been stripped of her HRH status after her divorce was draped in the Royal Standard on her final night at home.

I didn't light the candles until everyone had gone.

Then I sat on my chair, one hand on the coffin, one hand on the biblical text and prayers. While an estimated thirty thousand people prayed by candlelight in the gardens and parks outside, I was privileged to sit with Diana, Princess of Wales, surrounded by candles, and the heavy perfume of flowers.

I didn't want to dwell on prayers. I had said prayers all week with so many different friends. In the Chapel Royal. Below the Nelson Shanks portrait. At the foot of my bed. All I wanted to do was chat like we used to do.

So, as I said, I spent the night talking to the princess, and had one special conversation with her, never taking my hand off the lid of her coffin. In my mind, and because of her own spiritual beliefs, I felt she was in that room anyway, watching and listening, laughing and crying with me.

I had brought with me her A4-sized, hardback, green address book, embossed with a gold 'D' and a coronet. It was packed with the names of friends and associates from all walks of life. It was these people who had each played an important role in her life at one time or another, and each had a story to tell. Each one deserved to be remembered in his or her absence. My privileged position at the centre of the princess's world meant that I knew a story or had a memory about each friend.

So I sat there, from midnight until seven o'clock the next morning, going through that book, name by name, memory by memory, and each anecdote or story would often begin with the words 'Do you remember when . . .'

From the Arundels and Lord Attenborough to

Father Austin, the priest in Liverpool to whom she turned on many occasions for spiritual guidance. From Cindy Crawford to Kevin Costner. From the Lonsdales to the Lawsons. From Lord Mischcon to George Michael. From Wayne Sleep to Meredith Etherington-Smith. From Barbara Walters to Oprah Winfrey. All the way through the alphabet, ending with Sir Magdi Yacoub. There were more than a hundred names, but I didn't miss a single one. In that respect, although I was alone during that vigil, all the people she knew well said farewell to her that night.

For Lord Attenborough, I talked about the time when she had flown by helicopter to support him at a charity event, and how she had chuckled at the sight of him running across the field to greet her, then leading her, hand in hand, to the event.

James Colthurst was the middle man between the boss and Andrew Morton, and I reminded her of the double helpings he always had at their meals together, and how she had giggled at the amount he ate before he pedalled off on his bicycle.

For Elton John, I recalled that she'd spent a memorable evening at his home in Windsor when he had played his piano and serenaded her with some of her favourite songs.

I spoke of how the diminuitive Japanese masseur Madame Kubo had walked all over the boss's back, every Wednesday evening, with her bare feet, using her toes to manipulate her spine. 'Remember the cries of agony but how you said it did you the world of good?'

I remembered how Lord Rothschild used to make her day by sending her armfuls of long-stemmed, heavily scented pink carnations, which he had grown in his greenhouse.

As for her Californian friend Kenny Slutsky, there had been the hilarious time when he had sent her his gold American Express card so that I could go into London and purchase an authentic suit of armour which he wanted to stand in the hallway of his home overlooking Manhattan Beach. The stories—from the weird to the wonderful—were endless. There had been so many special times. I told her how lucky she had been to have had such people around her, and I told her about everyone outside, the flowers they had laid, and the mark she had made on ordinary people.

The next day, the world said farewell to Diana, Princess of Wales, in a service at Westminster Abbey, which was followed by a private family ceremony at Althorp. She was buried on the island in the middle of the lake. What nobody knows is that she had told me about that island, and how she had rowed on its waters as a child. In fact, she had shown me a photograph, taken on a winter's morning during a weekend visit in 1987. How eerie that, just ten years later, she was buried in the exact spot she had captured on camera.

I was one of nine people who stood on that island on 6 September 1997. At the end of a moving, thirty-minute ceremony, I picked up a handful of earth, crouched down and dropped it on to the brass plate bearing her name. 'Goodbye, Your Royal Highness,' I whispered.

*   *   *

The loss of the princess set in motion for me a chain of events over which I had little or no control. When she was alive, I seemed to be at the helm and everything was under control. But in death, I lost that control to outsiders who either knew best, wanted to usurp me or wanted to sideline the all-knowing—and some would say meddling—butler.

I was made redundant from the Diana, Princess of Wales Memorial Fund as its fund-raising manager but was proud to have played a significant part in helping to raise £100 million for charity in her name. I was then wrongly arrested by Scotland Yard who failed to understand the generosity, or the legacy, of the princess. Since then, of course, I've got back on my own two feet, gone public with the memories and insights of a life shared with the boss.

So much has changed in the past ten years. I've moved in a different direction without abandoning the memory of Diana, Princess of Wales. I'm moving on while still remembering and, regardless of the media's misrepresentation of my intentions to share memories and tributes with the rest of the world, I'll never stop shouting about how magical life was with the princess, and how we should not allow her spirit to be forgotten.

After all I have been through since her death, I recognize that every day is a perfect day.

Many people will speak and offer opinions about the princess in the coming weeks, months and the tenth anniversary year. I can only hope that what they say will either celebrate or vindicate her, not attempt to besmirch, discredit or cloud her memory.

My knowledge about the princess is vast. She entrusted much to me. And I know that I've been true to her memory. As I've always maintained, there are secrets and truths inside my head that will go with me to the grave. In paying tribute to the boss, I have protected a wealth of information, I can assure you. If she is still looking down on us all, she will know that more than anyone—however much those who are blind to the extent of my knowledge will attempt to speak on her behalf.

What I will say is that if people don't write it, history cannot be known.

This is my final book on Diana, Princess of Wales, to mark the tenth anniversary of her death.

In whatever I do and wherever life takes me next, I will be fortunate enough to carry with me the energy, influence and memory of one special lady who was my boss, friend, guide and inspiration. I'll never lose sight of what a privilege it was to serve at her side, and know her friendship.

And, if I dare borrow the words of someone else, I'd like to think I've been 'faithful, loyal, brave; friend more than servant—even to the grave . . .'

THANK YOU

The moment I met with publisher Trevor Dolby and we discussed the idea for this book, I knew we were on the same page, sharing a belief to celebrate the memory of Diana, Princess of Wales.

It takes vision, belief, and a degree of courage to back a book of this kind, and people like me rely on a strong team of talent to make such projects possible. I'm indebted to Trevor at HarperCollins, my agent Ali Gunn, of Gunn Media, for making it all happen, and for her constant faith and encouragement, and to Steve Dennis, my ghostwriter, who has worked tirelessly with me and been a real friend with his support, trust and guidance.

I would also like to thank:

The American publishers at HarperCollins USA: especially Lisa Gallagher and David Highfill; my US agent Alan Nevins in LA for your support; Deborah Schneider in New York, and Diana McKay in London; Chuck Webb and Ron Ruff in Florida—I don't know what I'd do without you both. Thanks also, once again, to my expert editor, Hazel Orme, whose eagle eye I couldn't have done without! Your polished contribution has been immeasurable. And not forgetting the rest of the team at HarperCollins UK, especially Managing Editor Kate Latham for co-ordinating everything in the background, Rose Harrow for all your assistance and Art Director James Annal for your stunning book cover, and not forgetting Belinda Budge, Lucy Vanderbilt, Eleanor Goymer, Jane

Beaton, Louise Edwards, Terence Caven and Rachel Smyth. And also Debbie Steer and Seale Ballenger in New York, plus all involved at HarperCollins US. Thanks also go to photographer Helen Turton for making me look good, and Jacks Thomas and Emma Lawson at Midas, in London, for all your advice.

This project, and others, have meant that I've spent a lot of time away from home this past year and I'd like to thank, more than anyone, my wife Maria, for her unstinting support and unconditional love. And thank you to my sons, Alex and Nick, for their love, and for contributing to this book with their memories of our special time at KP and Highgrove.

Finally, my heartfelt thanks and gratitude to the many thousands of people from around the world who have written to me with endless words of kindness and encouragement. Their letters sustain my belief that millions of people will never forget—and still want to remember—Diana, Princess of Wales.

Paul Burrell